HOUGHTON MIFFLIN HARCOURT

Texas JOURNEYS

Program Authors

James F. Baumann · David J. Chard · Jamal Cooks
J. David Cooper · Russell Gersten · Marjorie Lipson
Lesley Mandel Morrow · John J. Pikulski · Héctor H. Rivera
Mabel Rivera · Shane Templeton · Sheila W. Valencia
Catherine Valentino · MaryEllen Vogt

Consulting Author

Irene Fountas

Cover illustration by Valeria Docampo.

Copyright © 2011 by Houghton Mifflin Harcourt Publishing Company

Printed in the U.S.A.

ISBN 10:   0-54-724085-6
ISBN 13:   978-0-54-724085-5

23456789 - 0914 – 18 17 16 15 14 13 12 11 10

HOUGHTON MIFFLIN HARCOURT
School Publishers

Unit 1

Neighborhood Visit

Big Idea There are different kinds of communities.

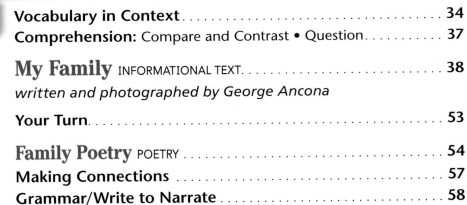

Unit 2

Nature Watch

Big Idea Nature can teach us many things.

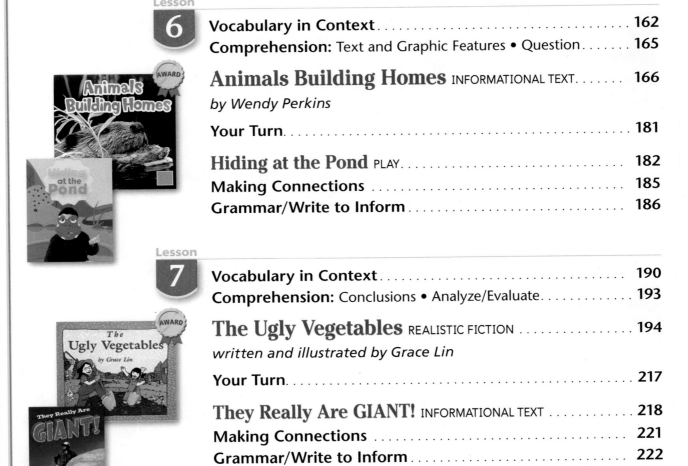

Unit 3

Tell Me About It

Big Idea We learn from each other.

Welcome, Reader!

You are about to begin a journey into reading. Along the way you will meet many new characters, such as a superhero dog. You'll also travel to the world of outer space and other exciting places. Your journey is sure to be filled with surprises, and you'll learn to be a better reader, too!

Get ready to meet some new friends with the story *Henry and Mudge*. Turn the page and let the fun begin!

Sincerely,

The Authors

Neighborhood Visit

Unit 1

Big Idea

There are different kinds of communities.

Paired Selections

✓ **TARGET VOCABULARY**

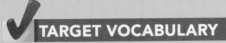

curly

straight

floppy

drooled

weighed

stood

collars

row

Vocabulary
Reader

Context
Cards

TEKS 2.5B use context to determine meaning;
ELPS 3D speak using content-area vocabulary

10

Vocabulary in Context

- Read each **Context Card**.

- Use a Vocabulary word to tell about something you did.

1
curly
A poodle is a dog that has very curly hair.

2
straight
Some kinds of dogs have long, straight hair.

3 floppy

Hound dogs have floppy ears. The ears hang down very low.

4 drooled

The Saint Bernard drooled all over the place!

5 weighed

A dog can be weighed on a scale. Then the vet knows how heavy the dog is.

6 stood

The dog stood still while it was measured.

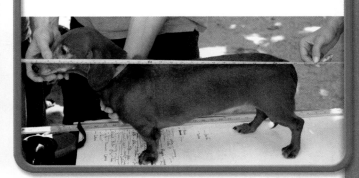

7 collars

Collars come in different styles. A collar goes around a dog's neck.

8 row

The dog treats are lined up in a row on the shelf.

Background

✓ TARGET VOCABULARY   **At the Animal Shelter**

If you want to adopt a dog, start at an animal shelter.
A shelter may have a row of dogs to choose from.
Some have dogs with curly fur or pointed ears. Shelters
have even had dogs that stood three feet tall! Play
with a few dogs before you choose one. Just be careful
not to get drooled on! After you get a new dog, take
it to a vet for an exam and to be weighed.

floppy ears

straight fur

collars

TEKS 2.3A use ideas to make/confirm predictions; **2.3C** establish purpose/monitor comprehension; **ELPS 4D** use prereading supports to comprehend texts

Comprehension

✔ TARGET SKILL Sequence of Events

In *Henry and Mudge,* one event happens, and then another and another. They follow in an order, or sequence, of events. Use a chart like the one below to show the sequence of the story events as you read.

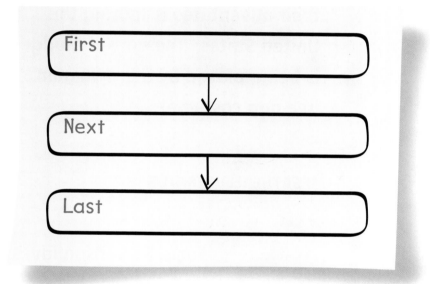

✔ TARGET STRATEGY Infer/Predict

Think about the sequence of story events and use what you already know. Make predictions about the story as you read *Henry and Mudge.* Then check to see if your predictions are correct.

JOURNEYS DIGITAL Powered by DESTINATIONReading
Comprehension Activities: Lesson 1

TARGET VOCABULARY

drooled	floppy
collars	stood
curly	straight
weighed	row

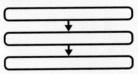
TARGET SKILL

Sequence of Events
Tell the order in which
things happen.

TARGET STRATEGY

Infer/Predict Use
clues to figure out more
about story parts.

GENRE
Realistic fiction is a
story that could happen
in real life.

MEET THE AUTHOR
Cynthia Rylant

Henry and Mudge have
starred in more than
twenty-five books
by Cynthia Rylant.
A musical based on
their adventures is touring the
United States. The part of Mudge
is being played by a grown man
in a dog costume!

MEET THE ILLUSTRATOR
Suçie Stevenson

Suçie Stevenson loves
drawing the character
of Mudge. In fact, she
has two big dogs of her
own. "They don't drool
as much as Mudge," she says.

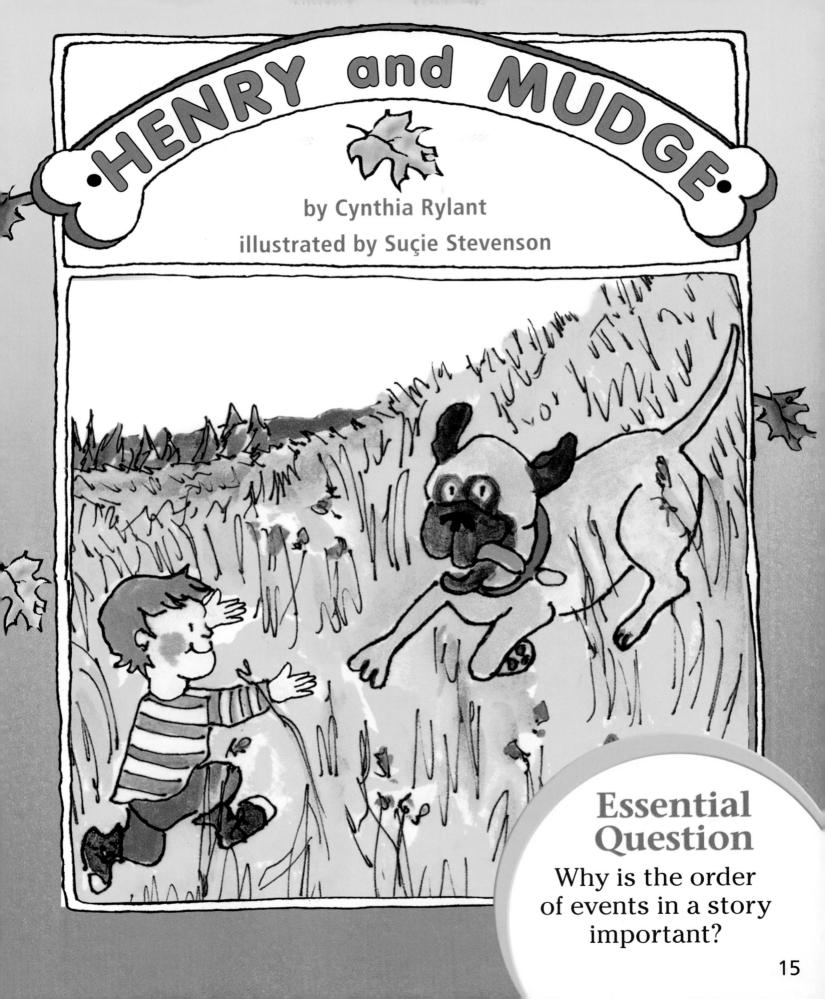

HENRY and MUDGE

by Cynthia Rylant

illustrated by Suçie Stevenson

Essential Question

Why is the order of events in a story important?

Henry had no brothers and no sisters.
"I want a brother," he told his parents.
"Sorry," they said.
Henry had no friends on his street.

"I want to live on a different street,"
he told his parents.
"Sorry," they said.
Henry had no pets at home.
"I want to have a dog," he told his parents.
"Sorry," they *almost* said.

✔️ STOP AND THINK
Infer/Predict What might Henry's parents
say about getting a dog?
Check your prediction as you read.
TEKS 2.3A

But first they looked at their house
with no brothers and sisters.
Then they looked at their street
with no children.
Then they looked at Henry's face.

Then they looked at each other.
"Okay," they said.
"I want to hug you!" Henry told
his parents.
And he did.

✔️ **STOP AND THINK**
Sequence of Events What
happened after Henry's parents
looked at each other?

19

Henry searched for a dog.
"Not just any dog," said Henry.
"Not a short one," he said.
"Not a curly one," he said.
"And no pointed ears."

Then he found Mudge.

Mudge had floppy ears, not pointed.

And Mudge had straight fur, not curly.

But Mudge was short.

"Because he's a puppy," Henry said.

"He'll grow."

STOP AND THINK

Author's Craft What words does the author use to describe Mudge?

And did he ever!
He grew out of his puppy cage.
He grew out of his dog cage.

He grew out of seven collars in a row.
And when he finally stopped growing . . .

he weighed
one hundred eighty pounds,
he stood three feet tall,
and he drooled.
"I'm glad you're not short,"
Henry said.
And Mudge licked him,
then sat on him.

24

Your Turn

1. Which word means the opposite of <u>curly</u>?
   - ⬭ tall
   - ⬭ short
   - ⬭ straight

   TEKS 2.5C

2. 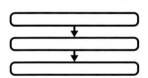 **TARGET SKILL** **Sequence of Events**
   What happens after Henry gets Mudge? Use a chart like this one to show what happens to Mudge. **TEKS** RC-2(E)

   ```
   ┌──────────────┐
   └──────────────┘
          ↓
   ┌──────────────┐
   └──────────────┘
          ↓
   ┌──────────────┐
   └──────────────┘
   ```

3. ✔ **TARGET STRATEGY** **Infer/Predict**
   Predict what you think Henry and Mudge will do next. Tell how you made your prediction. **TEKS** 2.3A, **ELPS** 4J

4. **Oral Language** Use the Retelling Cards to tell the beginning, middle, and end of the story. **TEKS** RC-2(E)

Retelling Cards

 TEKS **2.3A** use ideas to make/confirm predictions; **2.5C** identify/use antonyms/synonyms; **RC-2(E)** retell important story events; **ELPS** **4J** employ inferential skills to demonstrate comprehension

All in the Family

by Katherine Mackin

At the San Antonio Zoo, you can see many amazing animals. Some of these animals may have a family member living in your neighborhood!

Different Kinds of **Dogs**

Bush dogs live in Central America and South America. They have straight, brown fur. In the wild, they eat large rodents.

Pet dogs come in all shapes and sizes. They may have floppy ears or curly hair. They eat food made for dogs. Pet dogs should wear collars.

Cats of All Sizes

Lions belong to the cat family. They can grow up to eight feet long. Some have stood four feet tall. Lions hunt big animals in the wild.

Most house cats do not weigh more than fifteen pounds. They mostly eat special food for cats. However, some cats like to hunt for mice or birds.

27

Large Lizards

Komodo dragons are the largest lizards. They can grow to ten feet long. Some have weighed five hundred pounds! The saliva of a Komodo dragon is dangerous. You would not want to be drooled on by a Komodo dragon!

Little Lizards

Geckos belong to the lizard family. They are about eight inches long. Adult geckos weigh about one to two ounces. Geckos eat insects. They can eat ten crickets in a row.

Making Connections

 Text to Self TEKS 2.3B

Make a List Henry convinces his parents to get a dog. What reasons does he give? Imagine you want a new pet. List your reasons.

 Text to Text TEKS 2.30, ELPS 2D

Compare and Contrast With a partner, pick one of the animals from "All in the Family." Discuss how that animal is like and different from Mudge. Ask questions if you don't understand something your partner says.

 Text to World

Connect to Science Choose an animal from "All in the Family" to research. Make a list of questions and find the answers. Then share the answers with a partner.

 TEKS **2.3B** ask questions/clarify/locate facts/details/support with evidence; **2.30** follow discussion rules; **ELPS 2D** monitor understanding of spoken language/seek clarification

Grammar

Subjects and Predicates The **subject** of a sentence is the naming part. It tells who or what did or does something.

Academic Language

subject

predicate

Pam walks her dog.
The boy chooses a pet.

The **predicate** part of a sentence is the action part. It tells what the subject did or does.

The dogs pull on a rope.
Ben plays with his dog.

 **Write each sentence. Then circle the subject.**

❶ Mel grew tall.

❷ My father hugs the dog.

Write each sentence. Draw a line under the predicate.

❶ The boys play ball.

❷ Susan fed her dog.

Sentence Fluency When two short sentences have the same predicate, you can put the sentences together. Join them to make one longer sentence. Write *and* between the two subjects. This will make your writing smoother.

Short Sentences

Jim liked the park.

Spot liked the park.

New Sentence with Joined Subjects

Jim and Spot liked the park.

Connect Grammar to Writing

When you revise your sentences, try joining sentences that have the same predicate.

Write to Narrate

☑ **Ideas** Use details when you write a **true story** about something that happened. Details help your reader picture what you are telling about.

Megan drafted some sentences for a true story. See how she revised her writing to add details.

Writing Traits Checklist

☑ **Ideas**
Did I use details to tell the reader more?

☑ **Organization**
Did I tell about events in an order that makes sense?

☑ **Word Choice**
Did I use words that describe?

☑ **Voice**
Does my writing sound like the way I would tell the story?

Revised Draft

My friend Lucy gave me a beautiful
with many colorful beads
bracelet. She made it. She

calls it a friendship bracelet.

When I wear it I think of my

best friend Lucy.
I love my bracelet!

A Gift

by Megan Stiles

My friend Lucy gave me a beautiful bracelet. She made it with many colorful beads. She calls it a friendship bracelet. When I wear it I think of my best friend Lucy. I love my bracelet!

I added details to my final paper to make it more interesting.

Reading as a Writer

How do the words that Megan added help you picture what she is telling about? Where can you add details to your true story?

TARGET VOCABULARY

remembered

porch

crown

spend

stuck

visit

cousin

piano

Vocabulary
Reader

Context
Cards

TEKS 2.5B use context to determine meaning;
2.5D alphabetize/use dictionary/glossary

Vocabulary in Context

- Read each **Context Card**.

- Place the Vocabulary words in alphabetical order.

1
remembered
Mom remembered my birthday. She never forgets.

2
porch
They sat outside and talked on the front porch.

3 crown

This girl wears a crown on her head for her birthday.

4 spend

These girls spend time together. They play every day.

5 stuck

While on vacation, their car got stuck in the mud. It can't move.

6 visit

These grandparents like to visit. They see their grandchildren a lot.

7 cousin

My aunt and uncle have three children. Each child is my cousin.

8 piano

The father teaches his child to play the piano, a musical instrument.

Background

Family Visits What happens when families visit? Some families spend time sitting on a porch. Other families meet around a piano and sing songs. If someone gets stuck on the words, others help out. Many families gather for birthdays. The birthday boy or girl might wear a crown for the special day. No matter what a family does, the visit will be remembered for a long time!

grandfather

uncle

grandmother

cousin

aunt

mother

sister

father

me

TEKS **2.3B** ask questions/clarify/locate facts/details/support with evidence; **2.3C** establish purpose/monitor comprehension; **RC-2(C)** monitor/adjust comprehension; **ELPS** **4D** use prereading supports to comprehend texts; **4I** employ reading skills to demonstrate comprehension

Comprehension

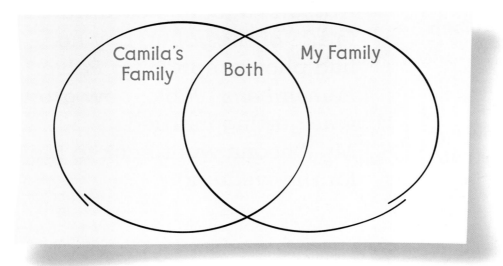

✔ **TARGET SKILL** **Compare and Contrast**

In *My Family,* you will find out how people in Camila's family are alike and different. As you read, use a Venn diagram like this one to compare and contrast details about Camila's family with your own family.

Camila's Family | Both | My Family

✔ **TARGET STRATEGY** **Question**

As you read, use your diagram to ask questions about how Camila's family members are alike and different. Questioning helps you understand what you read.

remembered	porch
crown	spend
stuck	visit
cousin	piano

Compare and Contrast Tell how two things are alike or not.

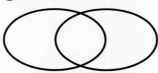

Question Ask questions about what you are reading.

GENRE
Informational text gives facts about a topic.

MEET THE AUTHOR AND PHOTOGRAPHER

George Ancona

George Ancona is often asked if he keeps in touch with the people he photographs. The answer is yes! Not long ago, he heard from the father of the young boy he had photographed for *Pablo Remembers*. Pablo, now grown, was getting married. Mr. Ancona went back to Mexico for the wedding.

My Family

by George Ancona

Essential Question

How are families alike and different?

I am Camila. I live in Miami with my
mother, Damaris, my father, Roberto, and my
brother, René. My mother came from Cuba.
My father came from Puerto Rico.

My mother and I go to school together. That's because she teaches Spanish in my school. When we are at home, I like to help her cook dinner.

Sometimes when my Grandma Marta comes to visit, I dress up and put on a show for her. Today she is teaching me a song. It goes like this:

There once was a sailor at sea
who liked to play the guitar.
When he remembered his far away land
he picked his guitar, and started to sing:
On the high sea, on the high sea, on the
high sea. [repeat]

René is my little brother. Our friends and
family come to the house for his birthday. We play
games, eat, and sing "Happy Birthday" to him.

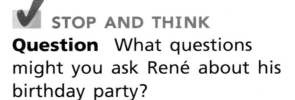 STOP AND THINK
Question What questions
might you ask René about his
birthday party?

Here is my family: Grandmother Marta and
Grandfather Rigoberto had four children. Almost
all of them came to René's birthday party.

Marta & Rigoberto

Andrés & Darleen	María Irene & Victor	Martica & Miguel	Damaris & Roberto	◄ They married:
Victor Mar Isabel	Victoria Valeria Vanesa	Gabriela Leticia	René Camila	And they had these children: ◄

Grandma came with Aunt María Irene and Victoria. Uncle Andrés came with Victor and Mar Isabel. Aunt Martica, Uncle Miguel, Gabriela, and Leticia came too. Soon the house was full.

We played many games. Aunt María Irene showed us how to play hopscotch. Little Leticia put on a crown to dance. Grandpa Rigoberto danced with cousin Mar Isabel.

On Sundays we go to church with Grandma.
Then we all go to Aunt Martica and Uncle Miguel's
house. After lunch we play music and sing.

Uncle Miguel plays the double bass. Uncle Andrés plays the violin. Aunt Darleen plays the piano. Victor plays the clarinet and Mar Isabel plays the flute.

STOP AND THINK
Author's Craft Music is part of Camila's story. Where in the story is music used?

We spend the rest of the day in the
backyard. The grown-ups play dominoes while
Uncle Andrés tells funny stories. Gabriela and I
sit on the porch and paint pictures.

 STOP AND THINK

Compare and Contrast How are the
activities of the adults the same as and
different from the activities of the
children on this page?

What I like best is when Papi takes us
fishing. Most of the time my hook gets stuck
on a rock. I can't wait to catch my first fish.

Your Turn

1. On page 47, the word <u>crown</u> means —

   ⬭ a special hat

   ⬭ a pretty dress

   ⬭ a loud horn

2. 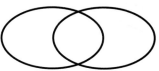 **TARGET SKILL** **Compare and Contrast**

   Show how the activities that the adults and children in Camila's family do are the same and different. **TEKS** 2.3B

3. ✔️ **TARGET STRATEGY** **Question**

   What questions did you have about Camila's musical family that were answered in the text? **TEKS** 2.3B, **ELPS** 4I

4. **Oral Language** Tell a partner some things you learned about Camila's family. Use the Retelling Cards. Be sure to speak clearly.
   TEKS 2.29, RC-2(E)

   Retelling Cards

 TEKS **2.3B** ask questions/clarify/locate facts/details/support with evidence; **2.29** share information/ideas by speaking clearly; **RC-2(E)** retell important story events; **ELPS 4I** employ reading skills to demonstrate comprehension

Poetry

Family
Poetry

remembered	stuck
porch	visit
crown	cousin
spend	piano

GENRE
Poetry uses the sound of words to show pictures and feelings.

TEXT FOCUS
Rhythm is a pattern of beats, like music.

Family Poetry

A family may have parents, brothers, sisters, grandparents, cousins, and more. People in a family visit one another and spend time together. Poets write about these remembered times. Listen to the rhythm of these family poems as you read them.

Everybody Says

Everybody says

I look just like my mother.

Everybody says

I'm the image of Aunt Bee.

Everybody says

My nose is like my father's.

But *I* want to look like ME!

by Dorothy Aldis

Abuelita's Lap

I know a place where I can sit
and tell about my day,
tell every color that I saw
from green to cactus gray.

I know a place where I can sit
and hear a favorite beat,
her heart and *cuentos* from the past,
the rhythms honey-sweet.

I know a place where I can sit
and listen to a star,
listen to its silent song
gliding from afar.

I know a place where I can sit
and hear the wind go by,
hearing it spinning round my house,
my whirling lullaby.

by Pat Mora

What is a family?

What is a family?

Who is family?

Either a lot or a few is a family;

But whether there's ten or there's two in *your* family,

All of your family plus you is family!

by Mary Ann Hoberman

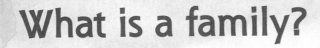

Write a Family Poem

What do you like to do with your family? Do you tell stories on the porch? Do you play the piano and sing? Write a poem about your family. Try to use the words crown and stuck in your poem.

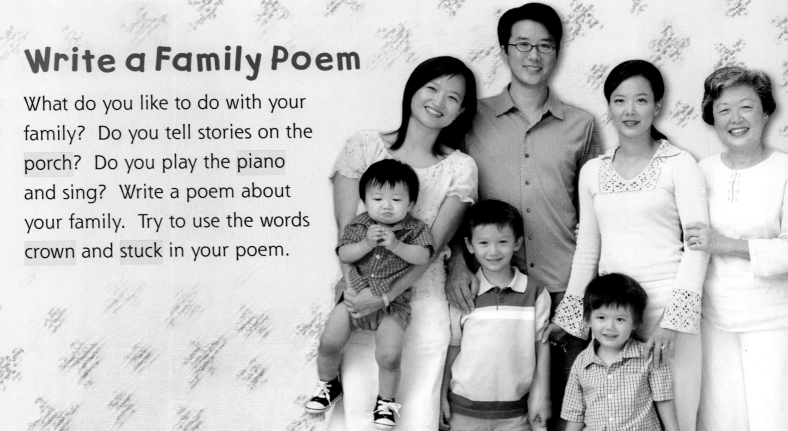

56

Making Connections

 Text to Self

Select an Activity What activity from *My Family* would you like to do with a family member? Explain your answer.

 Text to Text

Write About Families What is special about the families you have read about? Write a poem using what you have learned about families. Add details that tell about your senses.

 Text to World

Connect to Social Studies Camila's mother came from Cuba. Her father came from Puerto Rico. Now her family lives in Miami. Where could you look to find out more about these places? Make a plan.

 TEKS 2.18B write short poems using sensory details; **2.24B** determine relevant information sources; **RC-2(F)** make connections to experiences/texts/community; **ELPS 4G** demonstrate comprehension through shared reading/retelling/summarizing/responding/note-taking

Grammar

Complete Sentences A **sentence** has both a **subject** and a **predicate**. The subject tells who or what did or does something. The predicate tells what the subject did or does.

Academic Language

sentence
subject
predicate

Subject	Predicate
Ana	sings.
My older brother	plays the drums.

Turn and Talk **Work with a partner. Read each group of words aloud. Tell which groups of words are sentences.**

❶ Dad cooked.

❷ Harry's birthday.

❸ Ate three slices of cake!

❹ Jen and Bobbi danced.

Sentence Fluency When you write, use complete sentences. This will make your writing clearer.

Not Complete Sentences

My family.

Was Auntie Lu's birthday.

Complete Sentences

My family had a party. It was Auntie Lu's birthday.

Connect Grammar to Writing

When you revise your friendly letter, fix any sentences that are not complete. Add a subject or a predicate.

Write to Narrate

☑ **Voice** When you write a **friendly letter**, the voice of your letter shows what you are like.

Nestor drafted a letter to his uncle. Then he added words to make the letter sound more like the way he would talk to his uncle.

Writing Traits Checklist

☑ **Organization**
Did I use the five parts of a friendly letter? Did I tell things in order?

☑ **Word Choice**
Did I use words that tell how I feel?

☑ **Voice**
Does the letter sound like me?

☑ **Conventions**
Did I capitalize and punctuate the date, greeting, and closing correctly?

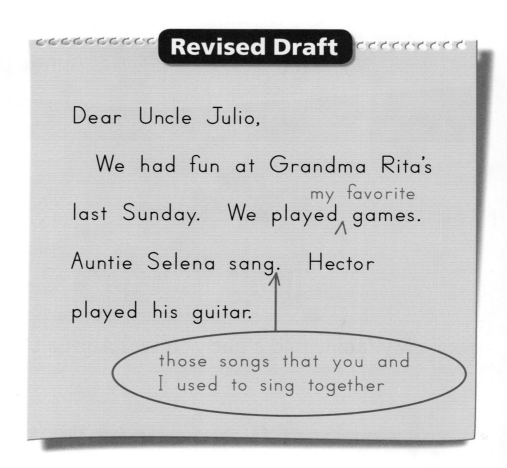

Revised Draft

Dear Uncle Julio,

We had fun at Grandma Rita's last Sunday. We played my favorite games.

Auntie Selena sang. Hector played his guitar.

those songs that you and I used to sing together

60

September 24, 2011

Dear Uncle Julio,

   We had fun at Grandma Rita's last Sunday. We played my favorite games. I wish you had been there. Auntie Selena sang those songs that you and I used to sing together. Hector played his guitar. Maybe you can come next time we go to Grandma Rita's. I miss you!

Love,
Nestor

> I added words so my letter sounds like me and shows how I feel.

Reading as a Writer

What did Nestor add to let you know how he feels? What can you add to your letter to show your thoughts and feelings?

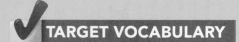

woods

turned

tops

chipmunks

busy

picked

south

grew

Vocabulary   Context
Reader   Cards

TEKS 2.5B use context to determine meaning;
ELPS 3D speak using content-area vocabulary

Vocabulary in Context

● **Read each Context Card.**

● **Talk about a picture. Use a different Vocabulary word from the one in the card.**

---

1 **woods**

It is fun to walk in the woods. There are trees all around.

---

2 **turned**

These leaves turned red in the fall. They changed color.

3 tops

The tops of these trees look like they are pointing to the sky.

4 chipmunks

Chipmunks have brown fur with white and black stripes.

5 busy

When you are busy, you have a lot to do.

6 picked

These children picked apples from the trees at an apple farm.

7 south

Many birds fly south for the winter. The weather is warmer there.

8 grew

This dog grew thicker fur for the winter. The thicker fur will keep the dog warm.

Background

✓ **TARGET VOCABULARY**   **A Busy Season**   In many areas, fall is a busy time. It begins even before the first tree tops have turned from green to orange. Birds fly south for the winter. Apples and pumpkins are picked. The woods are busy, too. Chipmunks store nuts. Some deer even shed the antlers that they grew in the spring.

64

Comprehension

✔️ TARGET SKILL Author's Purpose

The author has a purpose for writing *Henry and Mudge Under the Yellow Moon*. Fill in a chart like this one with details as you read. Use them as clues to decide why the author wrote the selection.

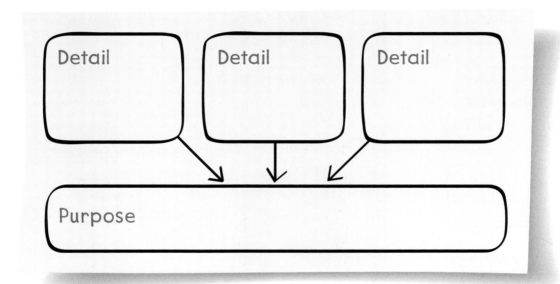

✔️ TARGET STRATEGY Analyze/Evaluate

Think carefully about the story details and the author's purpose for writing *Henry and Mudge Under the Yellow Moon*. Use your own ideas to decide if the author has done a good job of writing this story.

Main Selection

TARGET VOCABULARY

busy	turned
chipmunks	tops
south	grew
woods	picked

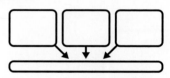
TARGET SKILL

Author's Purpose Tell why an author writes a book.

TARGET STRATEGY

Analyze/Evaluate Tell how you feel about the text, and why.

GENRE
Realistic fiction is a story that could happen in real life.

MEET THE AUTHOR
Cynthia Rylant

Cynthia Rylant loves animals, which is why you will find many in her books. She likes to take walks with her dogs. "Sometimes we have adventures," she says. "Someone will fall into a lake or someone will meet a raccoon— but mostly we just have lovely, quiet walks."

MEET THE ILLUSTRATOR
Suçie Stevenson

Suçie Stevenson has drawn the pictures for most of the Henry and Mudge books. Her brother's Great Dane, Jake, gave her the idea for Mudge. Suçie Stevenson takes her own dogs for walks on the beach. She likes seeing them swim to fetch balls.

HENRY and MUDGE
Under the Yellow Moon

by Cynthia Rylant

Illustrated by Suçie Stevenson

Essential Question

Why might an author write a story?

Together in the Fall

In the fall,
Henry and his big dog Mudge
took long walks in the woods.

Henry loved looking at
the tops of the trees.
He liked the leaves:
orange, yellow, brown, and red.

Mudge loved sniffing at the ground.
And he liked the leaves, too.
He always ate a few.

✔ **STOP AND THINK**
Author's Purpose Why does the author show that Henry and Mudge are good friends?

In the fall,
Henry liked counting the birds
flying south.
Mudge liked
watching for busy chipmunks.

Since one was a boy
and the other was a dog,
they never did things
just the same way.

73

Henry picked apples
and Mudge licked apples.

STOP AND THINK
Author's Craft How does having the
words **picked** and **licked** in the same
sentence make that sentence fun to read?

Henry put on a coat
and Mudge grew one.
And when the fall wind blew,
Henry's ears turned red
and Mudge's ears
turned inside out.

But one thing about them
was the same.
In the fall
Henry and Mudge liked
being together,
most of all.

✔ STOP AND THINK

Analyze/Evaluate Why do
you think Henry and Mudge
like to be together in the fall?

TEKS 2.3B

Your Turn

1. How is Henry different from Mudge?

   ⬭ Henry likes walks.

   ⬭ Henry likes leaves.

   ⬭ Henry picks apples.

   TEKS 2.9B

2. 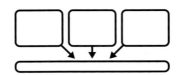 **TARGET SKILL** **Author's Purpose**

   What was the author's purpose for writing pages 73–75? Use a chart like this to list your ideas.

3. **TARGET STRATEGY** **Analyze/Evaluate**

   What is your favorite thing that Henry and Mudge do while they are in the woods? Explain using story details. **TEKS** 2.3B

4. **Oral Language** Using the Retelling Cards, take turns retelling the story with a partner. Listen carefully. **TEKS** 2.28A, 2.30, **ELPS** 2E

   Retelling Cards

TEKS **2.3B** ask questions/clarify/locate facts/details/support with evidence; **2.9B** describe characters' traits/motivations/feelings; **2.28A** listen/ask clarifying questions; **2.30** follow discussion rules; **ELPS 2E** use support to enhance/confirm understanding of spoken language

Technology

✔ TARGET VOCABULARY

woods	busy
turned	picked
tops	south
chipmunks	grew

GENRE

Informational text gives facts about a topic.

TEXT FOCUS

An **e-mail** is an electronic message sent from one person to another. As you read, find the different parts of an e-mail.

TEKS 2.16C identify written conventions for digital media

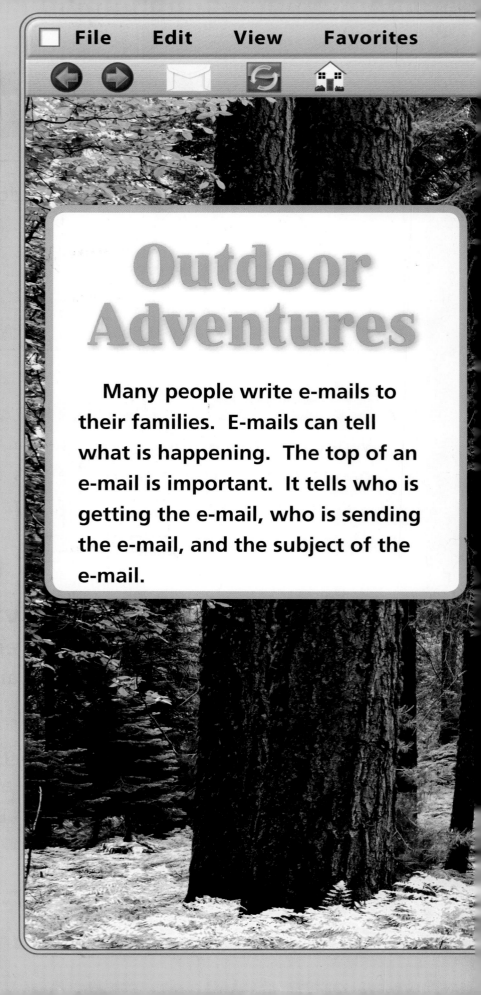

File   Edit   View   Favorites

Outdoor Adventures

Many people write e-mails to their families. E-mails can tell what is happening. The top of an e-mail is important. It tells who is getting the e-mail, who is sending the e-mail, and the subject of the e-mail.

search

To: Abuelita

From: Lola

Subject: Animal Hunt

Dear Abuelita,

   We are very busy in school this week. Each day we are walking in the woods. Today we found animals. We saw chipmunks storing acorns for the winter. I spotted a hare that already grew its winter coat. It was very furry! We also saw birds flying south. I took a picture for you.

Write back!

Lola

Geese fly in a V shape. They take turns flying in the front. This helps them fly longer.

File   **Edit**   **View**   **Favorites**   **Tools**   **Help**

To: Lola

From: Abuelita

Subject: Plant Hunt

Dear Lola,

   Your walks at school sound like fun. I have been taking walks, too. I look at plants in the woods. The tree tops have turned from green to red. Leaves cannot last through the cold winter. They are starting to drop off. I picked a few leaves to take home. Here are some pictures for you.

Talk to you soon,

Abuelita

Trees that have needles do not change colors. They can survive the winter.

When leaves turn colors, they stop making food for the tree.

Making Connections

ELPS 3G, 3H

 Text to Self

Describe an Activity Henry and Mudge loved walking in the leaves. Do you enjoy walking in the leaves? Describe to a partner what you like and don't like about it. Give specific details.

TEKS 2.3B, 2.9A

 Text to Text

Compare and Contrast Think about how the two *Henry and Mudge* stories you read are alike and different. Write sentences that tell what happens in each story. Tell how the settings are alike and different.

TEKS 2.24A

 Text to World

Connect to Science Go for a nature walk in your community. Draw and label interesting things you see. Make a list of questions you have about anything you see with a partner.

Maple Leaf

What makes leaves change from green to red?

 TEKS **2.3B** ask questions/clarify/locate facts/details/support with evidence; **2.9A** compare works by the same author; **2.24A** generate topics/formulate questions; **ELPS** **3G** express opinions/ideas/feelings; **3H** narrate/describe/explain with detail

Grammar

Statements and Questions Statements and questions are types of **sentences.** All sentences begin with a capital letter. A **statement** tells something. It ends with a period. A **question** asks something. It ends with a question mark.

Academic Language

sentences

statement

question

Statements	Questions
I live near the woods. Brendan sat by the pond.	Do you live near the woods? Who sat by the pond?

Try This! **Decide whether each sentence is a statement or a question. Write each sentence correctly.**

1. where do you like to walk

2. we hike up the hills

3. may I come with you

4. i will bring my jacket

Sentence Fluency Using different kinds of sentences makes your writing more fun to read. You can change one kind of sentence to another by moving or adding words.

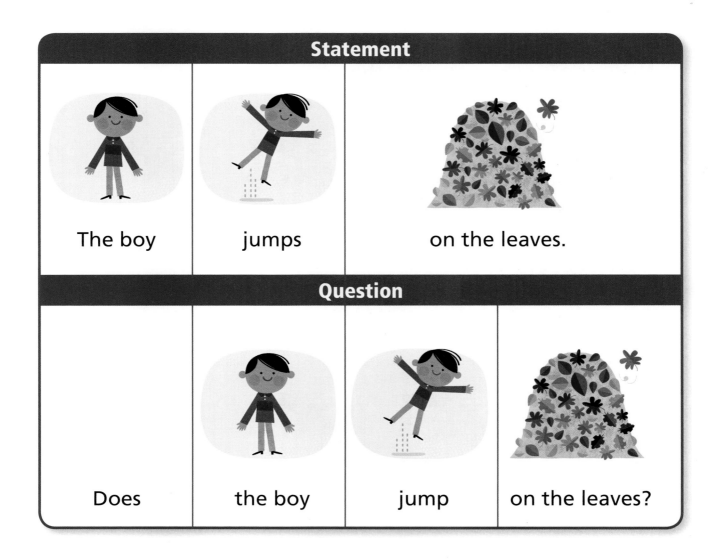

Statement		
The boy	jumps	on the leaves.

Question		
Does	the boy	jump	on the leaves?

Connect Grammar to Writing

When you revise your sentences that describe, try using different kinds of sentences to make your writing more interesting.

Write to Narrate

☑ **Word Choice** You can make a **description** more interesting when you use sense words to tell how things look, feel, smell, sound, and taste.

Nadia drafted a paragraph that describes where she lives. Later, she added sense words.

Writing Traits Checklist

☑ **Ideas**
Did I think of different ways to tell about where I live?

☑ **Organization**
Did I tell things in an order that makes sense?

☑ **Word Choice**
Did I use sense words to tell more?

☑ **Sentence Fluency**
Did I use different kinds of sentences?

Revised Draft

I live in a house near a lake.
little green   big blue

I love our house. You can see
the lake from our porch. The
I love to feel the warm
when it
sun comes in my bedroom

window in the morning.

My House

by Nadia Krimsky

I live in a little green house near a big blue lake. I love our house. You can see the lake from our porch. I love to feel the warm sun when it comes in my bedroom window in the morning. Do you know what wakes me up? The birds start chirping. I smell the pancakes my dad makes. They taste so good that I always ask for more!

I used sense words to tell the reader more about how things look, feel, smell, taste, and sound.

Reading as a Writer

Which sense words did Nadia add? What sense words can you add to your story?

4

✓ **TARGET VOCABULARY**

insects

dangerous

scare

sticky

rotten

screaming

breeze

judge

Vocabulary Reader	Context Cards

 TEKS 2.5B use context to determine meaning; **ELPS** 1E internalize new basic/ academic language; **3D** speak using content area vocabulary

Vocabulary in Context

- Read each **Context Card**.

- Ask a question that uses one of the Vocabulary words.

1 insects

Ants, flies, and bees are all insects. They all have six legs.

2 dangerous

Be careful! A bee sting can be dangerous. It makes some people sick.

3 scare

Cockroaches will run away if you scare them. They frighten easily.

4 sticky

A spider web is sticky. Bugs get caught, and they can't fly away.

5 rotten

A housefly eats rotten, or spoiled, food.

6 screaming

If you see a wasp, walk away quietly. Don't run away screaming.

7 breeze

A ladybug came in when a breeze blew open the window curtains.

8 judge

Look carefully before you judge, or decide, what this picture shows.

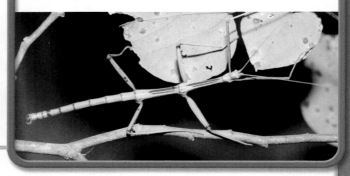

Background

✓ **TARGET VOCABULARY** **Spiders** Spiders are not insects. Spiders have eight legs. Insects have six. Some spiders spin sticky webs to catch food. Their webs are so strong a breeze will not break them. Spiders may scare people and cause a lot of screaming, but most are not dangerous. In fact, spiders are helpful because they eat harmful insects. They do not eat rotten things. Do not judge spiders based on the few that bite.

Crab Spider
(Heriaeus Hirtus)

feeler

eye

leg

Comprehension

✔ TARGET SKILL Cause and Effect

Some people see a spider and get scared. The two events are linked. Seeing the spider is the cause. Becoming scared is the effect. As you read, use a chart like this one to list some of the causes and effects in *Diary of a Spider*. Tell what happens and why.

Cause	Effect

✔ TARGET STRATEGY Summarize

Use your chart to help you summarize, or briefly retell in your own words, some important story events and their causes.

Main Selection

By Doreen Cronin · Pictures by Harry Bliss

DIARY OF A SPIDER

✔ **TARGET VOCABULARY**

insects	rotten
dangerous	screaming
scare	breeze
sticky	judge

Cause and Effect Tell how one event makes another happen.

✔ **TARGET STRATEGY**

Summarize Stop to tell important events as you read.

GENRE
Humorous fiction is a story that is written to make the reader laugh.

MEET THE AUTHOR

Doreen Cronin

Two spiders have moved into Doreen Cronin's office, but she says she cannot bring herself to get rid of them. If you like *Diary of a Spider*, check out Ms. Cronin's other books, *Diary of a Worm* and *Diary of a Fly*.

MEET THE ILLUSTRATOR

Harry Bliss

Whenever Harry Bliss visits classrooms, he asks students to scribble on the board. He then turns their scribbles into an animal, a tree, or a cartoon character. This scribble game helps kids use their imagination.

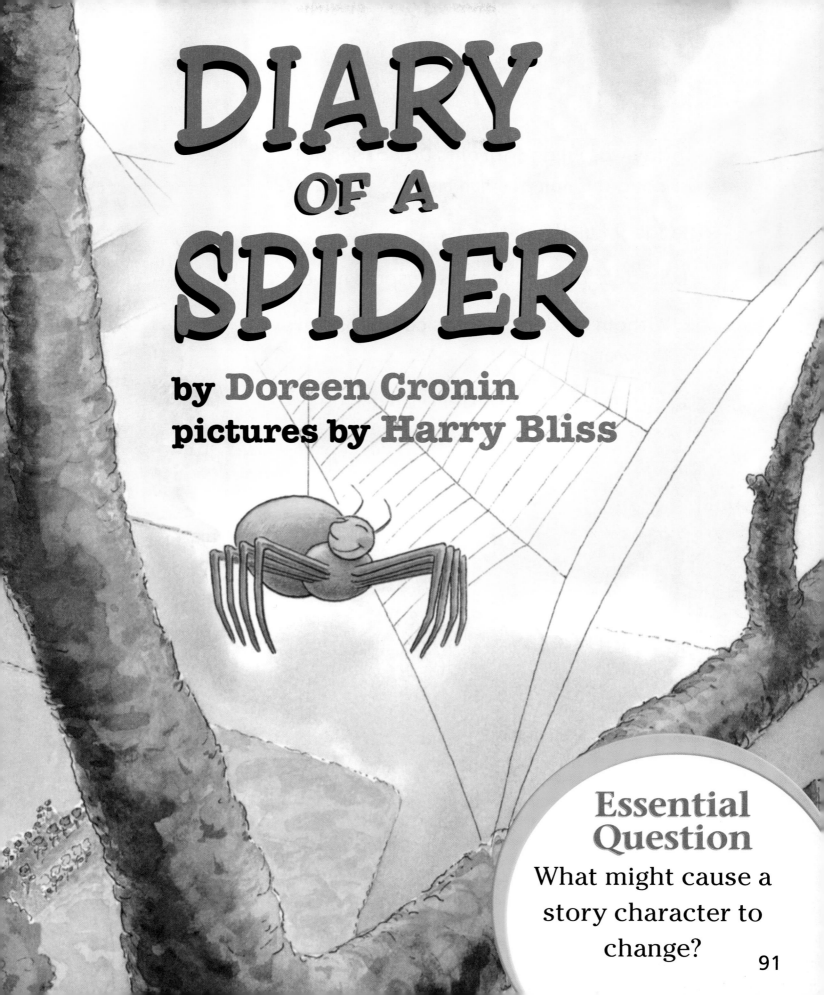

DIARY OF A SPIDER

by **Doreen Cronin**
pictures by **Harry Bliss**

Essential Question

What might cause a
story character to
change?

MARCH 1

Today was Grandparents Day at school, so
I brought Grampa with me.

He taught us three things:

1. Spiders are not insects—insects have six legs.

2. Without spiders, insects could take over
   the world.

3. Butterflies taste better with a little
   barbecue sauce.

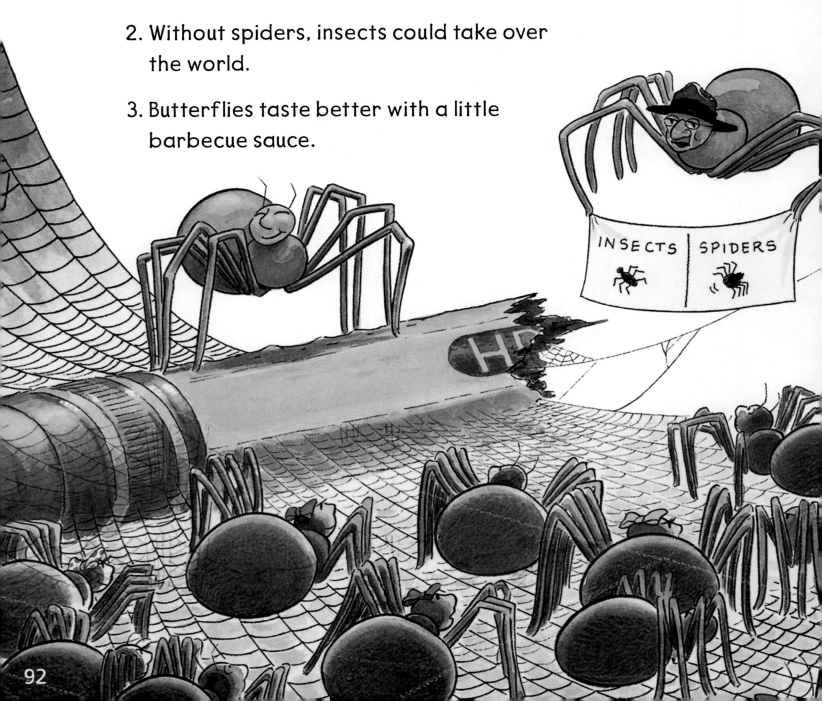

MARCH 16

Grampa says that in his day, flies and spiders did not get along.

Things are different now.

MARCH 29

Today in gym class we learned how to catch the wind so we could travel to faraway places.

When I got home, I made up flash cards so I
could practice:

1. Climb high.

2. Release silk.

3. Catch wind.

Fly made up her own flash card:

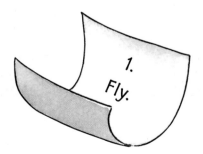

1. Fly.

I'm starting to see why
Grampa doesn't like her.

✔ STOP AND THINK

Summarize What does Spider do
to learn to fly to faraway places?

TEKS 2.3C, RC-2(C)

APRIL 1

I went to the park with my sister today. We tried the seesaw.

It didn't work.

✔️ **STOP AND THINK**
Cause and Effect Why does the seesaw not work? Use the illustration to help you answer.

96

We tried the tire swing.

It didn't work.

We spun a huge sticky web on
the water fountain.

That worked.

EEEEEEEK!

APRIL 12

Today was Safety Day at school. We learned that vacuums eat spiderwebs and are very, very dangerous. If we hear a vacuum, we should Stop, Drop, and Run.

APRIL 13

We had a vacuum drill today.
I stopped what I was doing.

Forgot where I was going.

And ran screaming from the room.

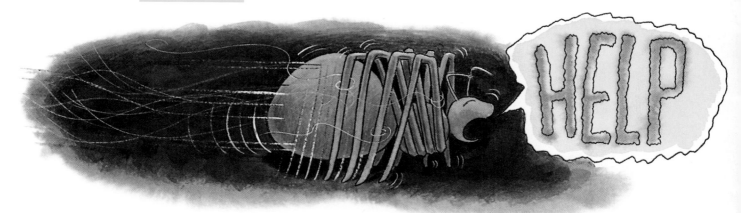

We're having another drill tomorrow.

APRIL 17

I'm sleeping over at Worm's house tonight. I hope they don't have leaves and rotten tomatoes for dinner again.

MAY 7

Mom said I was getting too big for my own skin. So I molted.

That is soooo gross!

MAY 8

Today was show-and-tell. So I brought in my old skin. My teacher called on it to lead the Pledge of Allegiance.

JUNE 5

Daddy Longlegs made fun of Fly because she eats with her feet. Now she won't come out of her tree house.

I'm going to find him and give him a piece of my mind!

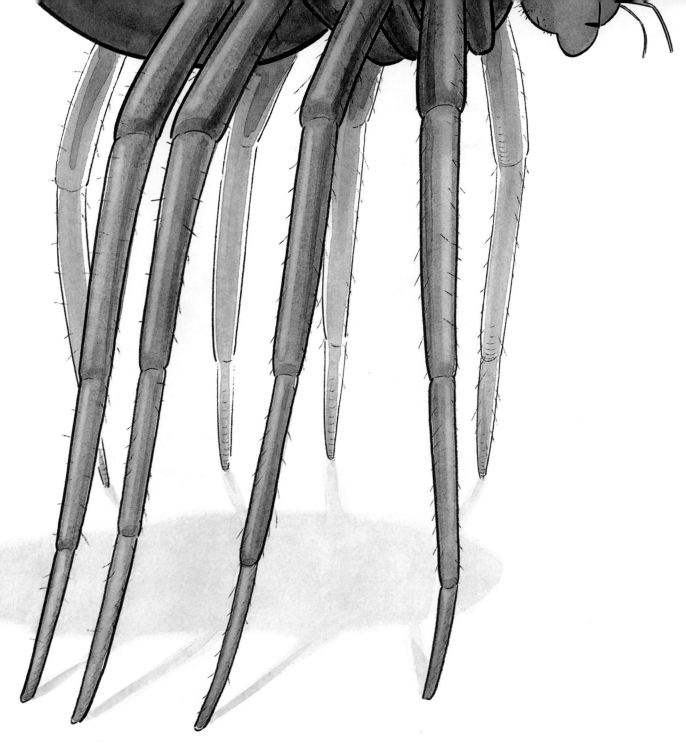

JUNE 6

I found Daddy Longlegs. He's a lot bigger than I thought he was.

I gave him a piece of my lunch instead.

JUNE 7

Fly's tree house blew away in the wind today.

So did Grampa.

JUNE 18

I got a postcard from Grampa today:

Dear Spider,
Ooh-la-la!
I landed in Paris!
French bugs are
delicious!
        Au revoir,
            Grampa

leg of French gnat...
give it a try!

Spider
5 Web Ave.
Arachnidville
05400
USA

JUNE 30

Grampa came home today. I couldn't wait to hear about how he rode the winds all the way over the ocean!

Turns out, he caught a breeze to the airport and napped in first class.

JULY 2

Fly came over to play today. She got stuck in our web, and her mom had to come get her.

Grampa laughed a little too hard.

From now on, we have to play at Fly's house.

106

JULY 9

Today was my birthday. Grampa decided I was old enough to know the secret to a long, happy life:

Never fall asleep in a shoe.

JULY 16

Things I scare:

1. Fly's mom

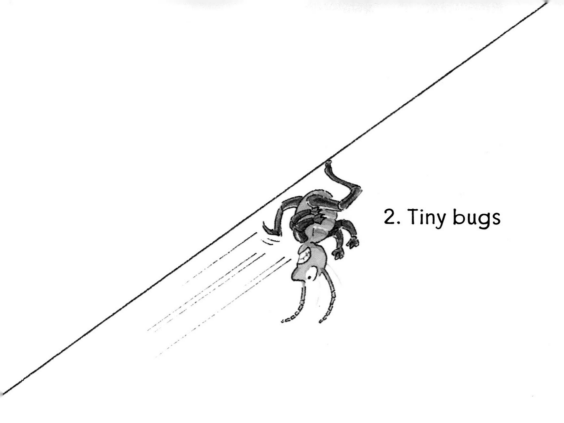

2. Tiny bugs

3. People using water
   fountains at the park

JULY 17

Things that scare me:

1. Daddy Longlegs

2. Vacuums

3. People with big feet

AUGUST 1

I wish that people wouldn't judge all spiders based on the few spiders that bite.

I know if we took the time to get to know each other, we would get along just fine.

Just like me and Fly.

STOP AND THINK

Author's Craft The story is funny because Spider seems like a person. How does the author make Spider seem like a person?

TEKS 2.9B

Your Turn

1. On page 105, the word <u>breeze</u> means —
   - ⬭ a big spider
   - ⬭ a light wind
   - ⬭ an airplane

2. 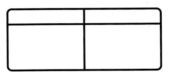 **TARGET SKILL** **Cause and Effect**

   What things cause Spider to be scared? Why? Use a chart like this to answer the question. **TEKS** 2.9B, **ELPS** 4J

3. ✔ **TARGET STRATEGY** **Summarize**

   Use your chart to help you summarize important story events and their causes. **TEKS** 2.3B, **ELPS** 4J

4. **Oral Language** Work with a partner or small group. Use the Retelling Cards to act out the story. **TEKS** RC-2(E), **ELPS** 4F

Retelling Cards

 TEKS **2.3B** ask questions/clarify/locate facts/details/support with evidence; **2.9B** describe characters' traits/motivations/feelings; **RC-2(E)** retell important story events; **ELPS** **4F** use visual/contextual/peer/teacher support to read/comprehend texts; **4J** employ inferential skills to demonstrate comprehension

113

Traditional Tales

✔ **TARGET VOCABULARY**

insects	rotten
dangerous	screaming
scare	breeze
sticky	judge

GENRE

A **fable** is a short story in which a character learns a lesson.

TEXT FOCUS

The **moral** of a fable is the lesson that a character learns. As you read, find the moral of the story.

 TEKS 2.6A identify moral lessons in well-known tales

Readers' Theater

A SWALLOW AND A SPIDER

A FABLE FROM AESOP

retold by Sheila Higginson

Cast of Characters

Narrator   **Spider**   **Swallow**

〰〰〰〰〰〰〰〰〰〰〰〰〰〰〰

Narrator: A spider sat in her sticky web, waiting for dinner.

Spider: I hope some insects will stop by soon.

Narrator: Spider heard the buzz of flies floating in the breeze.

Swallow: Look at those juicy flies!

Narrator: Before the flies could reach her web, they were scooped up in Swallow's beak.

Spider: Swallow is a pest! I will show him what I can do!

Narrator: Spider worked for a whole week. She spun a huge web.

Spider: Swallow doesn't scare me. I may be small, but I am dangerous, too!

Narrator: Spider put some berries in the middle of the web.

Spider: Swallow will smell these berries. Then he will get stuck in my net!

Narrator: Spider watched and waited, waited and watched.

Swallow: I smell something delicious. Those berries are just waiting for me!

Spider: Those berries aren't for you! Don't eat them! They are rotten.

Narrator: Swallow scooped up the berries and flew right through spider's web! He didn't even hear spider screaming at him!

Spider: I can judge what I am good at. I am good at building webs to catch insects, but I am not a good bird-catcher. I'll go back to my web to wait for a juicy fly.

Narrator: The moral of the story is, "A wise man will not try something he is not able to do."

Making Connections

 Text to Self TEKS 2.8

Different Ending Think about how *A Swallow and a Spider* could have ended differently. Write the new ending as a play and act it out.

 Text to Text TEKS 2.9B, ELPS 4J

Compare and Contrast *Diary of a Spider* and *A Swallow and a Spider* are both about spiders. Make a list of ways they are alike and different.

 Text to World TEKS 2.3B, ELPS 4J

Connect to Science Make a poster to teach your classmates about real spiders. Use the two stories you just read or science books to help you.

 TEKS **2.3B** ask questions/clarify/locate facts/details/support with evidence; **2.8** identify/use dialogue in plays; **2.9B** describe characters' traits/motivations/feelings; **ELPS** **4J** employ inferential skills to demonstrate comprehension

Grammar

What Is a Noun? A **noun** is a word that names a person, animal, place, or thing.

Academic Language

noun

People	Animals
grandfather girl friend	spider fly bird

Places	Things
home school park	web vacuum tomato

Turn and Talk **Work with a partner. Find the noun in each sentence. Tell whether it is a person, animal, place, or thing.**

❶ Our swing did not move.

❷ The worm sleeps.

❸ My teacher is nice.

❹ The airport is big.

Word Choice When you write, use exact nouns to paint a picture in your reader's mind. An exact noun gives more information about an animal, a person, a place, or a thing.

Noun	Exact Nouns		

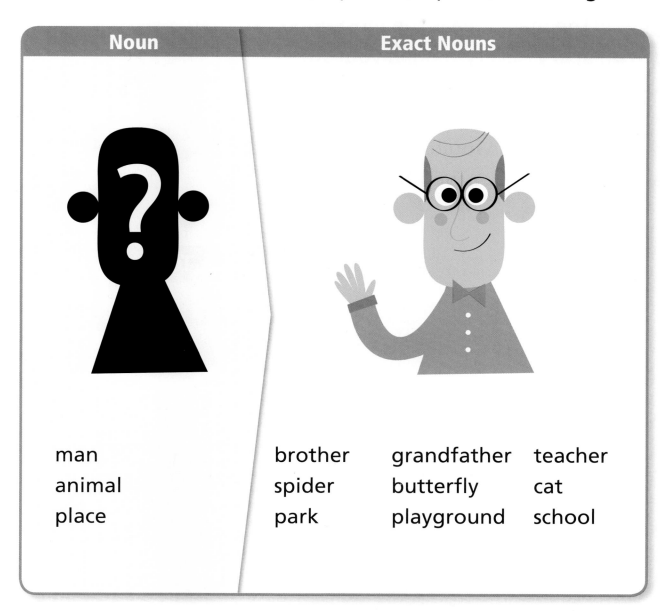

man	brother	grandfather	teacher
animal	spider	butterfly	cat
place	park	playground	school

✎ Connect Grammar to Writing

As you revise your true story next week, look for nouns you could replace with exact nouns.

119

Reading-Writing Workshop: Prewrite

Write to Narrate

✓ **Ideas** The main idea is the most important part of a **true story**. Everything in your story should connect to the main idea.

Raj made a list of ideas for his true story. He decided which idea would make the best story. Then he made an idea web for his true story.

Writing Process Checklist

▶ **Prewrite**

☑ **What is the most important idea of my story?**

☑ **What details tell about what happened?**

☑ **Do all the parts of the story connect to the main idea?**

☑ **Is there anything that doesn't belong?**

Draft

Revise

Edit

Publish and Share

Exploring a Topic

basketball

my sister's cat

video games

⟮ me in the author's chair ⟯

why I don't like to practice piano

120

Idea Web

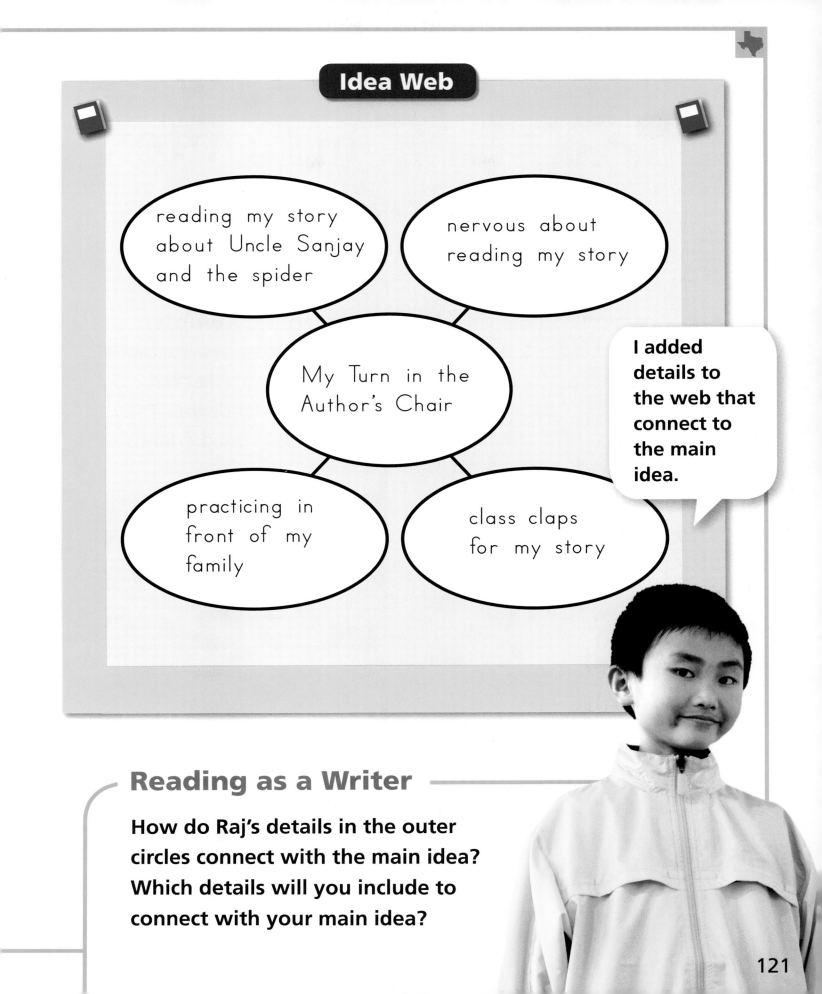

reading my story about Uncle Sanjay and the spider

nervous about reading my story

My Turn in the Author's Chair

practicing in front of my family

class claps for my story

I added details to the web that connect to the main idea.

Reading as a Writer

How do Raj's details in the outer circles connect with the main idea? Which details will you include to connect with your main idea?

Teacher's Pets

See Westburg by Bus!

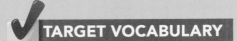

TARGET VOCABULARY

wonderful

noises

quiet

sprinkled

share

noticed

bursting

suddenly

Vocabulary Reader

Context Cards

 TEKS 2.5B use context to determine meaning

Vocabulary in Context

- Read each **Context Card**.

- Tell a story about two pictures, using the Vocabulary words.

1 wonderful

Pets are wonderful. They make very good friends.

2 noises

Big dogs bark loudly. Small dogs do not make such loud noises.

3 quiet

A lizard is a very quiet pet. It does not make a sound.

4 sprinkled

The fish food was lightly sprinkled on top of the water.

5 share

These kittens all share a bowl of food.

6 noticed

This pet rabbit noticed, or looked carefully, at the carrot held for it to eat.

7 bursting

Look at this crowded basket. It is bursting with puppies!

8 suddenly

A pet parrot might surprise you if it suddenly says a word.

Background

✓ **TARGET VOCABULARY** **Classroom Pets** Which animals make the quietest classroom pets? They are not birds. Birds make loud noises. The classroom can be quiet, and suddenly a pet bird is bursting into song. They are not guinea pigs. When they run around, their wheels squeak and their cages rattle. The quietest pets are fish. They are so quiet they may not get noticed. Fish quietly eat food sprinkled in their tank. Why not share the classroom with wonderful pet fish?

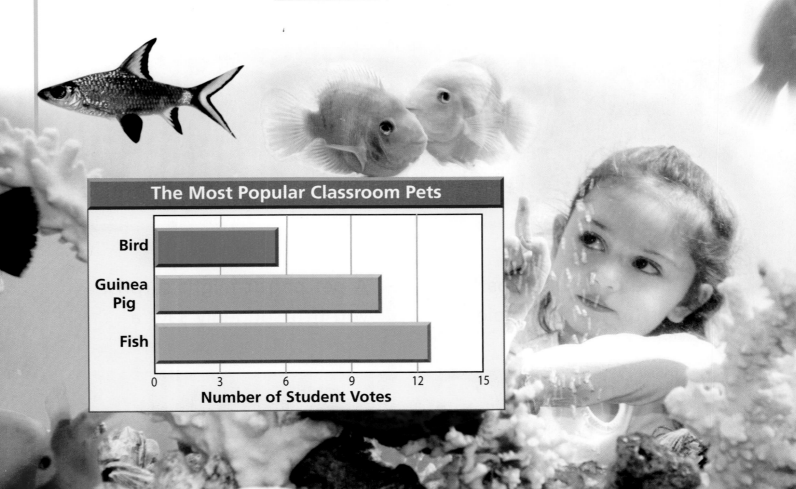

The Most Popular Classroom Pets

Number of Student Votes

Comprehension

✔ TARGET SKILL Story Structure

Where does *Teacher's Pets* take place, and who is in it? What problem does a character face, and how is it solved? Use a story map like this one to tell the main parts of the story. List details about the setting, characters, and plot.

Characters	Setting
Plot	

✔ TARGET STRATEGY Visualize

Visualizing, or drawing pictures in your mind, makes stories come to life. Use story details to visualize what happens at different parts of the story.

Teacher's Pets
Dayle Ann Dodds
Illustrated by Marylin Hafner

✔ TARGET VOCABULARY

wonderful	share
noises	noticed
quiet	bursting
sprinkled	suddenly

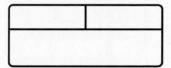

✔ TARGET SKILL

Story Structure Tell the setting, characters, and plot in a story.

✔ TARGET STRATEGY

Visualize Picture what is happening as you read.

GENRE

Realistic fiction is a story that could happen in real life. Set a purpose for reading based on the genre.

 TEKS **2.3C** establish purpose/monitor comprehension

126

MEET THE AUTHOR
Dayle Ann Dodds

Dayle Ann Dodds received a very special honor in 2007. Her book *Teacher's Pets* was read to hundreds of kids on the lawn of the White House during the annual Easter egg roll.

MEET THE ILLUSTRATOR
Marylin Hafner

Readers of *Ladybug* magazine know two characters created by Marylin Hafner, Molly and her cat, Emmett. For fun Ms. Hafner designs rubber stamps, usually with kids or animals on them.

Teacher's Pets

by Dayle Ann Dodds
illustrated by Marylin Hafner

Essential Question

What clues tell you where and when a story takes place?

127

Monday was sharing day in Miss Fry's class.

"You may bring something special," said Miss Fry.

"May we share a pet?" Winston asked.

"Yes," said Miss Fry. "But just for the day."

On Monday, Winston brought in his pet rooster.

"I call him Red. He eats corn, and he crows. The neighbors say he crows too much."

"What a wonderful pet," said Miss Fry. "We're happy he can visit us today."

But that afternoon, after all the children had left, there was Red, still sitting on his roost near Miss Fry's desk.

She sprinkled corn in Red's dish, then locked the door and went home to her quiet little house.

On Tuesday, Winston told Miss Fry, "The neighbors wonder if Red can stay at school for a while."

"Of course," said Miss Fry. "How lucky for us."

The next Monday was Patrick's turn. "My tarantula's name is Vincent. He likes to eat bugs and hide inside my mother's slippers."

"What a wonderful pet," said Miss Fry. "Don't forget to take Vincent home with you at the end of the day."

STOP AND THINK
Author's Craft What does "pet" mean above? What else can "pet" mean, as in a "teacher's pet"?
TEKS 2.5B, 2.11

132

But that afternoon, after all the children had left, there was Vincent, still sitting in his jar on Miss Fry's desk. She gave Vincent a big juicy bug, sprinkled corn on Red's dish, then locked the door and went home to her quiet little house.

On Tuesday, Patrick told Miss Fry, "My mother says Vincent likes her slippers too much. We're wondering if he can stay at school for a few days."

"Of course," said Miss Fry. "How lucky for us."

The next week, Roger brought in his cricket.

"His name is Moe," said Roger. "He eats leaves from the garden and sings *chirrup-chirrup* all night long."

"What a wonderful pet," said Miss Fry.

That afternoon, after all the children had left, Miss Fry noticed Moe sitting in his box on the table. Miss Fry looked at Moe. He almost seemed to smile. "Welcome to our class, Moe."

STOP AND THINK

Story Structure How does Winston start a big change in Miss Fry's classroom?

TEKS 2.3B

Right before her eyes, he did a huge somersault—up, up in the air. "Bravo!" said Miss Fry.

She gave fresh green leaves to Moe and a big juicy bug to Vincent, sprinkled corn in Red's dish, then locked the door and went home to her quiet little house.

The next day, Roger said to Miss Fry, "My mother says Moe chirps too much."

"He's welcome to visit as long as he likes," said Miss Fry.

And so it went.

Alia shared her pet goat named Gladys. It said *Baaaaa!* and ate her sister's homework.

Amanda shared her pet dachshund. It liked to chew bones and the pillows on her aunt Judy's new sofa.

Jerry brought in his pet boa constrictor. It never made a sound. No one knew exactly what it liked to eat, but Jerry said his father's expensive tropical fish had suddenly disappeared one day.

There was Megan's cat,

Mitchell's mice,

Daniel's ducks,

and Tom's iguana.

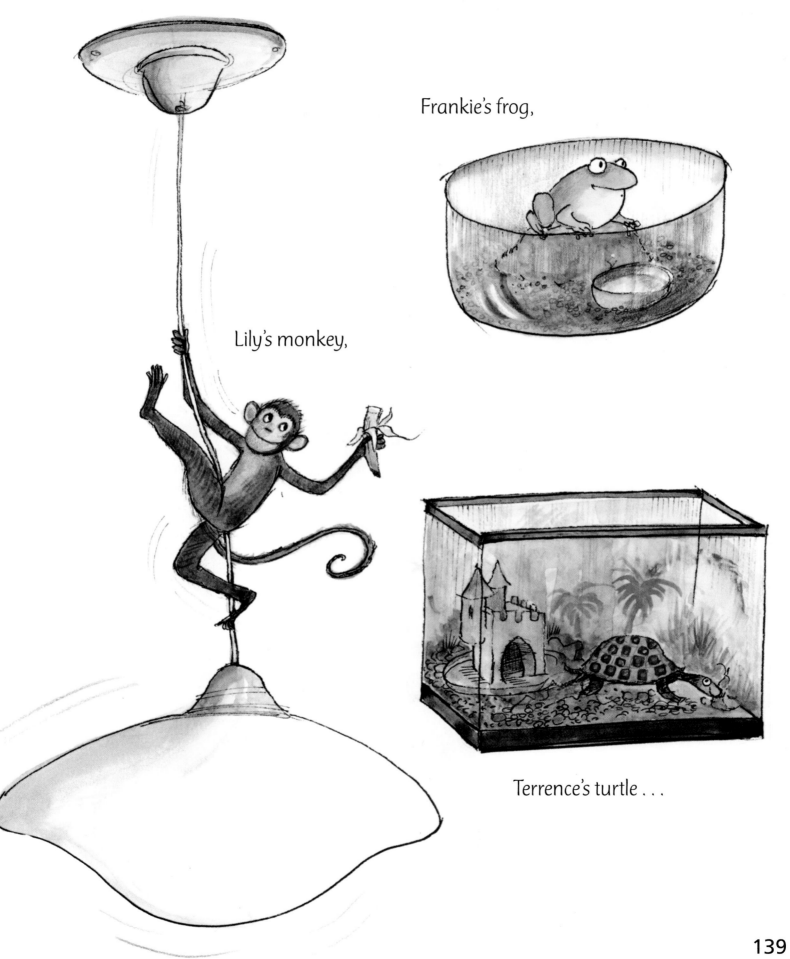

Frankie's frog,

Lily's monkey,

Terrence's turtle . . .

139

and something square and fuzzy that Avery brought in.

"It looks like a kitchen sponge," said Bruce. "A *really old* kitchen sponge."

"It's my pet," said Avery, and that was that.

Before long, Miss Fry's classroom was bursting with the happy noises of all the children's pets.

STOP AND THINK
Visualize All the animals are making sounds at once. What picture do you get in your mind of what is happening behind Miss Fry's door?
TEKS RC-2(C)

On Parents' Night, the mothers and fathers walked around
the classroom with great big smiles on their faces.

"Isn't it great," they said, "that Miss Fry loves pets so?"

Only Roger's cricket sat quietly in his box.

"You must miss your garden," Miss Fry said.

Chirrup, said Moe softly. He crawled under one of his shiny green leaves.

143

145

TEKS 2.3B ask questions/clarify/locate facts/details/support with evidence; 2.29 share information/ideas by speaking clearly; RC-2(E) retell important story events; ELPS 4J employ inferential skills to demonstrate comprehension

That night, Miss Fry opened her window.

See Westburg
by Bus!

✓ **TARGET VOCABULARY**

wonderful	share
noises	noticed
quiet	bursting
sprinkled	suddenly

GENRE

Informational text gives facts about a topic. This is a pamphlet.

TEXT FOCUS

A **map** is a drawing of a town, state, or other place.

See Westburg by Bus!

BUS

Welcome to Westburg!

The best way to see our town is on Bus Number 33. Get the bus in front of our Welcome Center. After you get on board, read this pamphlet. Just follow the numbers sprinkled on the map as you go.

We are happy to share our wonderful town with you.

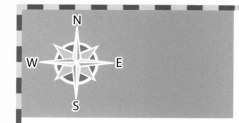

SILVER RIVER

Brown Street

Red Street

2 LIBRARY

Blue Avenue

Pine Street

3
Rainbow Park

1 WELCOME CENTER

1 Welcome Center
Find the Welcome Center. It is **bursting** with pamphlets, maps, and books about Westburg.

2 Library
The Public Library is on Blue Avenue. The children's room is a great place for books, computer games, and movies.

3 Rainbow Park
Cross Blue Avenue to get to Westburg's largest park. People come here to play, walk, or have some **quiet** time.

Key
river   bus route ■ ■ ■ ■ bridge

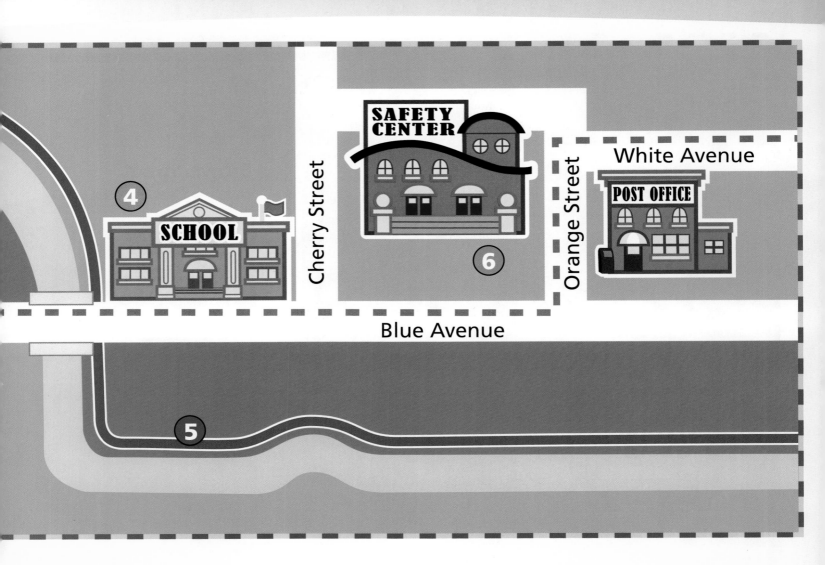

4 School

Take the bridge across the Silver River. When you get on the other side, Chávez Elementary will be on your left.

5 Bike Path

Have you noticed how the bike path follows the curves of the Silver River? What a great view!

6 Safety Center

If you suddenly hear siren noises as you pass the Safety Center, a fire truck or ambulance may be whizzing by!

Making Connections

 Text to Self

Write About School If you were a student in Miss Fry's class, what pet would you bring to school? Write to explain. Share your ideas with a partner.

 Text to Text   TEKS 2.25A, 2.25C

Connect to Math Would you rather spend a day in Miss Fry's room or a day in Westburg? Vote with the children in your class. Record the votes on a chart and find the difference.

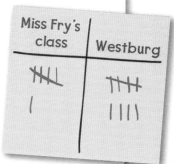

 Text to World   TEKS 2.25A, ELPS 4I

Research an Animal Choose a pet from the story *Teacher's Pets* that you would like to know more about. Research how to care for that type of pet.

 TEKS 2.25A gather evidence from sources/expert interviews; 2.25C record information in visual formats; ELPS 4I employ reading skills to demonstrate comprehension

Grammar

Singular and Plural Nouns A **singular noun** names one person, animal, place, or thing. A **plural noun** names more than one person, animal, place, or thing. Add -*s* to most nouns to name more than one.

Academic Language

singular noun

plural noun

Sentences with Singular Nouns	Sentences with Plural Nouns
The teacher talks loudly.	The two teachers talk to their students.
This playground looks big.	All playgrounds are fun.

Turn and Talk **Work with a partner. Read the sentences aloud. Name the singular nouns and plural nouns.**

❶ Two crickets sat in a cage.

❷ My friend has three cats.

❸ Her bird ate some seeds.

❹ Our teacher loves pets!

154

Conventions Edit your writing carefully. Make sure you have written nouns that name more than one in the correct plural form.

Singular Nouns	Plural Nouns
one frog a turtle	two frogs many turtles

Connect Grammar to Writing

When you edit your true story, be sure to write the correct form of all plural nouns.

TEKS 2.17B develop drafts; 2.17E publish/share writing; 2.18A write brief stories; 2.21A(vii) understand/use time-order transition words; **ELPS** 5G narrate/describe/explain in writing

Reading-Writing Workshop: Revise

Write to Narrate

☑ **Sentence Fluency** When you write a **true story**, use time-order words to let your reader know when things happened.

Raj drafted a story about the day he read a story to the class. Later, he added time-order words to tell when things happened.

Writing Process Checklist

Prewrite

Draft

▶ **Revise**

☑ Does my story have a beginning, middle, and end?

☑ Does the beginning make the reader want to read more?

☑ Did I use time-order words to tell when things happened?

☑ Does the ending wrap things up?

Edit

Publish and Share

Revised Draft

Last week it
I~t~ was my turn for the

Author's Chair. I chose my

story about Uncle Sanjay
                    At first
and the spider. I was
            Then ∧
nervous. ∧I practiced in

front of my family.

156

My Day
in the Author's Chair
by Raj Bhatti

Last week it was my turn for the Author's Chair. I chose my story about Uncle Sanjay and the spider. At first I was nervous. Then I practiced in front of my family. Finally I read the story to the class. I read the part about how Uncle Sanjay screamed when he saw the spider. The class laughed.

> I used time-order words to tell when things happened.

Reading as a Writer

What time-order words does Raj use to tell when things happened? What time-order words can you add to your true story?

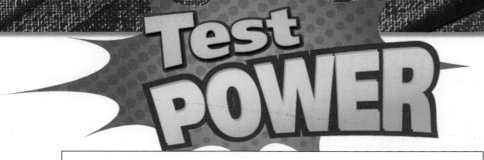

The King's Woods

1   Long ago, an old man lived deep in the King's woods. One day the prince rode through the woods. He saw the old man and shouted, "Get out of my woods!"

2   The man went to pack his things. Then he saw a sad sight. The prince's horse had fallen. The prince was <u>injured</u>. The old man ran to get help.

3   When the prince was better, he called for the old man. "You saved my life," he said. "You may have anything you want."

4   "I only want to stay in the woods," the man replied. And so he did.

GO ON

1 What happened after the man went to pack his things?

◯ The prince told the man to get out of the woods.

◯ The prince called for the old man.

◯ The prince's horse fell.

2 When does this story take place?

◯ In the future

◯ Today

◯ Long ago

3 What does the word <u>injured</u> mean in paragraph 2?

◯ Happy

◯ Hurt

◯ Inside

GO ON ➡

A Birthday Surprise

1   Mom was baking a cake. "It's for Mrs. Lopez's birthday," Mom said. "She is eighty-one years old today." Carlos liked Mrs. Lopez. She had some trouble seeing, but it never slowed her down. He wanted to do something special for her.

2   Then he got a <u>superb</u> idea. He got a book and went next door. "Surprise, Mrs. Lopez!" he said. "I'm going to read to you."

3   "I love to listen to you read," she said.

1 Why is Mom baking a cake?
- ⬭ It is Carlos's birthday.
- ⬭ It is Mrs. Lopez's birthday.
- ⬭ Carlos asked her to.

2 The word <u>superb</u> in paragraph 2 means –
- ⬭ great
- ⬭ old
- ⬭ silly

3 What did Carlos do first in the story?
- ⬭ Carlos got an idea.
- ⬭ Carlos read to Mrs. Lopez.
- ⬭ Carlos got a book.

STOP

Nature Watch

Unit 2

Big Idea

Nature can teach us many things.

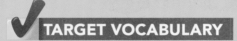

✔ **TARGET VOCABULARY**

shaped

branches

pond

beaks

deepest

break

hang

winding

Vocabulary
Reader

Context
Cards

 TEKS 2.5B use context to determine meaning; **ELPS** 4C develop/comprehend basic English vocabulary and structures

Vocabulary in Context

● **Read each Context Card.**

● **Use a Vocabulary word to tell about something you did.**

1
shaped
Have you ever seen a home shaped like this? It is curved like a ball.

2
branches
Tree branches high above the ground are a good home for a sloth.

3 pond

Turtles make their home in a **pond**, or small lake.

4 beaks

These birds use their **beaks** to build their home.

5 deepest

The **deepest** part of the ocean is this eel's home.

6 break

This home won't **break**! It is made of strong rock.

7 hang

These bats **hang** upside down in their cave.

8 winding

Some animal homes have long, **winding** tunnels that twist and turn.

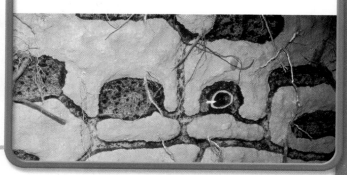

Background

✔ TARGET VOCABULARY **Animal Homes** Some birds build their homes with their beaks. Some insects build nests shaped like balls. They hang from branches. Often bats live in the deepest parts of caves. A frog may live by a pond. A clam lives in a shell that other animals cannot break easily. A groundhog digs a burrow that has winding tunnels. No matter where it lives, an animal feels safe in its home.

Hornet ▶
Hornets build nests in tree branches.

◀ Honey Bee
Honey bees live in hives. Inside the hives bees store honey.

TEKS 2.3B ask questions/clarify/locate facts/details/support with evidence; 2.13 identify topic/explain author's purpose; 2.14B locate facts in text; 2.14D use text features to locate information; ELPS 4I employ reading skills to demonstrate comprehension

Comprehension

✔ TARGET SKILL   Text and Graphic Features

The author chose the title, *Animals Building Homes*, to tell you the topic, or what the book is about. She also chose words, headings, and photos to make her ideas clear. Use a chart like this to list some features. Then tell why you think the author used them.

Text or Graphic Feature	Page Number	Purpose

✔ TARGET STRATEGY   Question

Think of the questions you have about how animals build their homes. Then look for some answers by reading the text and studying the graphic features in the article.

Main Selection

shaped	deepest
branches	break
pond	hang
beaks	winding

✔ **TARGET SKILL**

Text and Graphic Features Tell how words go with photos.

✔ **TARGET STRATEGY**

Question Ask questions about what you are reading.

GENRE
Informational Text gives facts about a topic.

MEET THE AUTHOR

Wendy Perkins

Can you guess why Wendy Perkins has been called a "walking animal encyclopedia"? It's because her mind is filled with facts and information about all kinds of animals.

Ms. Perkins has written nonfiction books about animal eyes, ears, feet, feathers, noses, teeth, and tails. She also writes articles for *Highlights for Children* and a magazine put out by the San Diego Zoo called *Zoonooz*.

Animals Building Homes

by Wendy Perkins

Essential Question

How can chapter headings help you?

A Beaver's Home

A beaver is hard at work. It gnaws on a tree trunk. Soon, the tree falls. The beaver floats the log to a pond. There, the beaver builds a **lodge**. The beaver piles up logs. It fills the cracks between the logs with mud and grass. The lodge keeps the beaver safe and warm.

Safe at Home

Most animals need a home. Homes keep animals safe from **predators**, rain, snow, or the hot sun. Some animals live in their homes for life. Other animals live in their homes long enough to raise their **offspring** or **survive** hot or cold weather.

 **STOP AND THINK**

Text and Graphic Features
Why are some of the words in dark print?

Building Nests

Many animals live in nests. A hummingbird builds a small cup-shaped nest. The nest is made of moss and bits of spiderweb.

A mouse makes a grass nest in the shape of a ball. The mouse hides its nest in tall grass or in a tunnel under the ground.

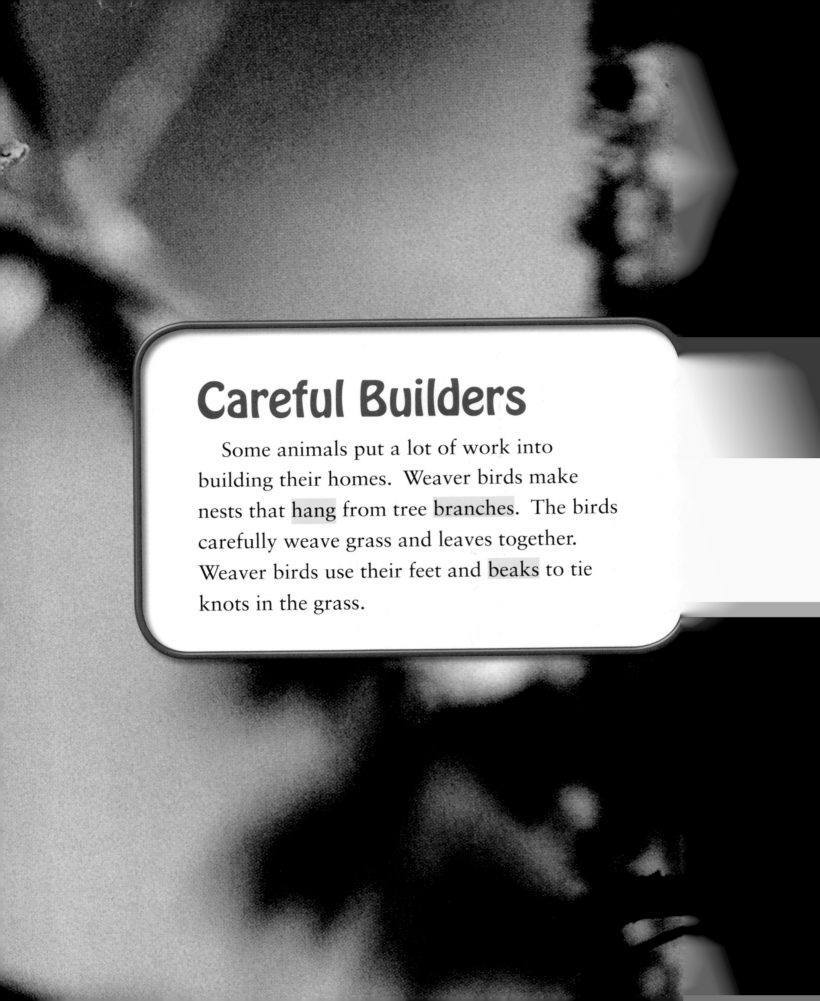

Careful Builders

Some animals put a lot of work into building their homes. Weaver birds make nests that hang from tree branches. The birds carefully weave grass and leaves together. Weaver birds use their feet and beaks to tie knots in the grass.

Working Together

Animals can work together to build homes. Termites build **mounds** made out of mud mixed with **saliva**. Other animals cannot easily break through the hard mud.

 STOP AND THINK

Question What question about how termites work together does this page answer?

TEKS 2.14B

Polyps are animals that make coral reefs. A polyp builds a **limestone** cup around its body for protection. The cups of the polyps grow together to make a coral reef.

Making a Burrow

Burrows are holes in the ground where some animals live. Gophers use their teeth and paws to dig long, winding tunnels. They make rooms in the deepest parts of the tunnels. The gophers hide their offspring and food in these rooms.

Home Improvement

Some animals live in homes made by other animals. Chickadees use tree holes made by woodpeckers. Chickadees bring grass and moss into the hole. They build a nest for their chicks.

STOP AND THINK

Author's Craft Why does the author name this page "Home Improvement"?

Building a Home

   Most animals need homes where they can rest and raise their offspring. Homes also keep animals safe from predators. Beavers build lodges. Mice make nests. Gophers dig burrows. How does a polar bear make its **den**?

1. The word <u>pond</u> on page 169 means a —
   - ⬭ small lake
   - ⬭ big river
   - ⬭ swimming pool

2. 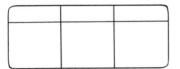 **TARGET SKILL** **Text and Graphic Features**

   List the features in *Animals Building Homes.* Then tell how they helped you understand the author's ideas.

   TEKS 2.3B, 2.14D, **ELPS** 4F

3. **TARGET STRATEGY** **Question**

   Look back at page 178. Write one question you have about the gopher. **TEKS** 2.3B

4. **Oral Language** Use the Retelling Cards to tell how some animals build their homes. Include facts and details.

Retelling Cards

 TEKS **2.3B** ask questions/clarify/locate facts/details/support with evidence; **2.14D** use text features to locate information; **ELPS 4F** use visual/contextual/peer/teacher support to read/comprehend texts

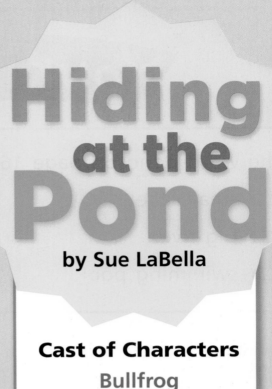

Hiding at the Pond

by Sue LaBella

Cast of Characters
Bullfrog
Snapping Turtle
Walking Stick

Bullfrog: (jumping) What a great day to jump! I'll hop along this winding path around the pond.

Walking Stick: Watch out for the snapping turtle.

Bullfrog: (stops and looks around) Who said that?

Walking Stick: I did.

Bullfrog: (looking around) I can't see you.

Walking Stick: Look closely at the tree branches. I'll hang down and wiggle.

Bullfrog: You look like a stick!

Walking Stick: That's right. I'm a bug called a walking stick. I have a stick-shaped body. It's great camouflage. Birds think I'm a twig, so they don't grab me with their beaks.

Bullfrog: My brown and green colors help me hide in the grass and in the pond.

Snapping Turtle: But not on the path!

Bullfrog: (surprised) Your dark color hides you well.

Snapping Turtle: I know. It hides me in the mud and in the deepest part of the pond, too.

Bullfrog: Your jaws look strong. Can they break things in half?

Snapping Turtle: Yes.

Bullfrog: (jumping away) Yikes! Bye!

Making Connections

 Text to Self   **TEKS** RC-2(F)

Share Experiences Think about the animal homes in *Animals Building Homes*. Which have you seen before? Share your ideas.

 Text to Text   **TEKS** 2.15A, 2.24B, **ELPS** 4J

Explore Homes at Ponds Work with a team to list animals from each selection that live in or near a pond. Discuss how these animals are alike and different. Name sources you might use to find more information.

 Text to World   **TEKS** 2.3B, 2.24A

Connect to Science What else would you like to learn about animal homes? Choose a topic to research. Find other texts, such as reference books, about your topic. Read the texts to locate facts about your topic. Ask questions to help you clarify, or understand, the information in the texts.

 TEKS 2.3B ask questions/clarify/locate facts/details/support with evidence; **2.15A** follow written directions; **2.24A** generate topics/formulate questions; **2.24B** determine relevant information sources; **RC-2(F)** make connections to experiences/texts/community; **ELPS** 4J employ inferential skills to demonstrate comprehension

Grammar

More Plural Nouns A **plural noun** names more than one person, animal, place, or thing. Add -s to most nouns to name more than one. Add -es to nouns that end with s, x, ch, and sh.

Academic Language

plural noun

Singular Nouns	Plural Nouns
one fox	two foxes
the class	many classes
a finch	some finches
the dish	three dishes

 **Read each sentence. Write the plural of each underlined noun.**

❶ The <u>boss</u> was angry.

❷ The beaver used a <u>bunch</u> of wood.

❸ This <u>bush</u> is heavy!

❹ The squirrel hid in a <u>box</u>.

186

Sentence Fluency You may join two short sentences with the same predicate to make one longer sentence. Write **and** between the two subjects. Your writing will be smoother.

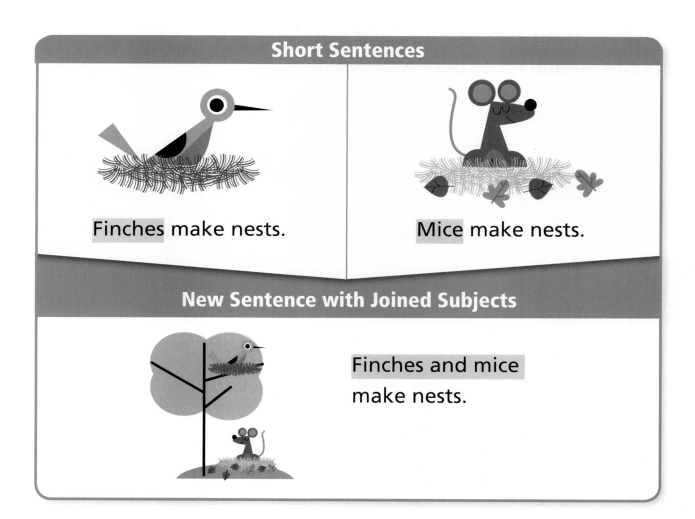

Short Sentences

Finches make nests.

Mice make nests.

New Sentence with Joined Subjects

Finches and mice make nests.

Connect Grammar to Writing

When you revise your writing, try joining two short sentences that have the same predicate.

Write to Inform

☑ **Ideas** When you write an **informational paragraph**, make sure you include details that tell about the main idea.

Sean drafted a paragraph about beaver homes. Later, he added more details about his main idea.

Writing Traits Checklist

☑ **Ideas**
Do all my details support the main idea?

☑ **Organization**
Does my topic sentence tell the main idea?

☑ **Word Choice**
Did I use exact words?

☑ **Conventions**
Did I write neatly and leave margins?

Revised Draft

They use parts of trees to build their homes there. Beavers live on ponds. ∧A beaver can use its teeth to

Then the tree falls. gnaw on a tree.∧

Beaver Lodges

by Sean McDonald

Beavers live on ponds. They use parts of trees to build their homes there. A beaver can use its teeth to gnaw on a tree. Then the tree falls. Beavers float logs to a place to build a lodge. The beaver uses mud and grass to fill cracks. That makes the lodge warm.

I added more details about beavers' homes.

Reading as a Writer

Which details did Sean add to tell more about his main idea? Where can you add details to your own paragraph?

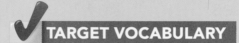

✓ TARGET VOCABULARY

blooming

shovels

scent

tough

wrinkled

plain

muscles

nodded

Vocabulary Reader | Context Cards

TEKS 2.5B use context to determine meaning;
ELPS 4D use prereading supports to comprehend texts

Vocabulary in Context

- Read each Context Card.

- Make up a new sentence that uses a Vocabulary word.

1 blooming

Sunflowers are blooming in the field. They face the sun as their flowers grow.

2 shovels

These children use shovels to help plant a tree.

3 scent

Roses have a scent, or smell, that is as sweet as perfume.

4 tough

A pumpkin has a tough outer skin that is hard to break.

5 wrinkled

A raisin is a dried, wrinkled grape, but it is still sweet.

6 plain

The plant on the left is plain. The plant on the right is fancy.

7 muscles

It takes strong muscles to use a loaded wheelbarrow.

8 nodded

The girl nodded her head up and down to show that she would help in the garden.

Background

Growing a Garden A flower garden has blooming flowers. Their scent fills the air. A vegetable garden looks plain, but it has plants to eat. Gardens take work. Gardeners need strong muscles to turn the soil with shovels. They plant seeds, and soon wrinkled sprouts unfold. When tough weeds grow, gardeners pull them up. If you have ever asked if gardening is hard work, the gardener will surely have nodded yes!

The flowers in this garden needed a lot of water to grow.

Comprehension

✔ TARGET SKILL Conclusions

As you read *The Ugly Vegetables*, use story clues to figure out more about the events and characters. Use clues to draw conclusions, or make smart guesses, about what the author does not say. Write the clues you use and a conclusion in a chart like this.

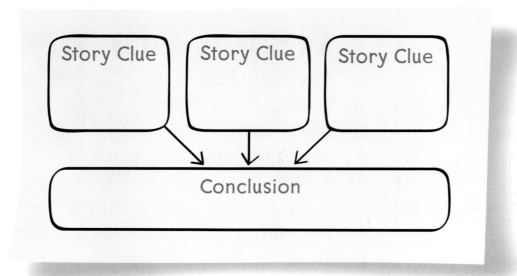

✔ TARGET STRATEGY Analyze/Evaluate

As you read, think carefully. Do your conclusions help you understand the story? Do you learn more about gardening? Use your conclusions to decide how you feel about *The Ugly Vegetables*.

✔ TARGET VOCABULARY

blooming	wrinkled
shovels	plain
scent	muscles
tough	nodded

✔ TARGET SKILL

Conclusions Use details to figure out more about the text.

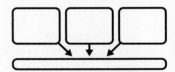

✔ TARGET STRATEGY

Analyze/Evaluate Tell how you feel about the text, and why.

GENRE

Realistic fiction is a story that could happen in real life.

MEET THE AUTHOR AND ILLUSTRATOR

Grace Lin

The Ugly Vegetables tells the true story of something that happened to Grace Lin when she was little. The book caused a big problem in her family because she didn't include her two sisters in it.

They made her promise to put them in her other books, which she has done. *Dim Sum for Everyone* and *Kite Flying* are about a family with three girls, just like the Lin family.

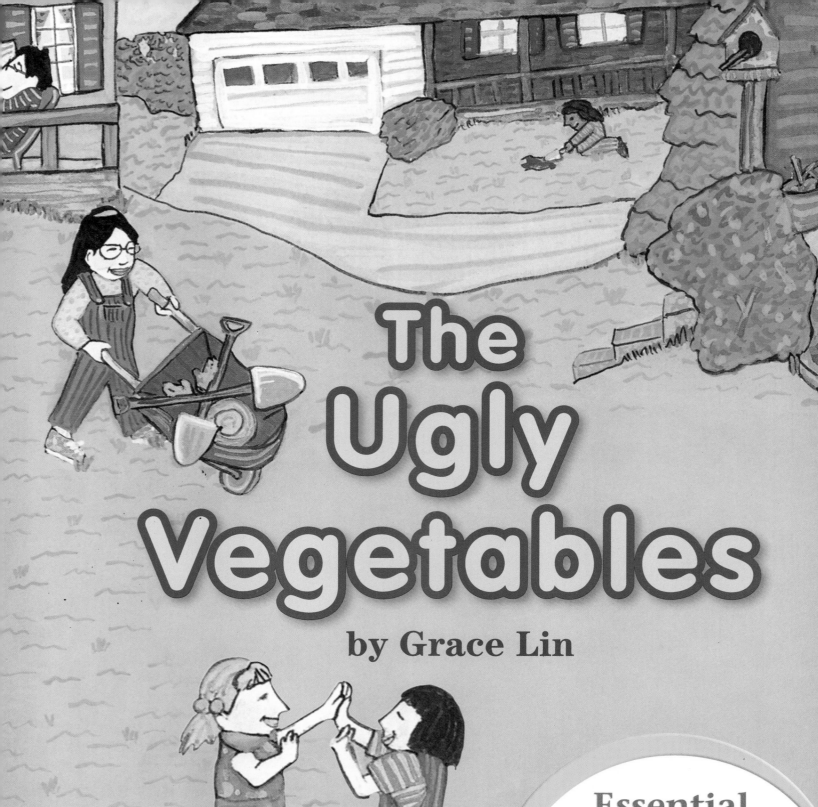

The Ugly Vegetables

by Grace Lin

Essential Question

What helps you make decisions about a character?

195

In the spring I helped my mother start our garden. We used tall shovels to turn the grass upside down, and I saw pink worms wriggle around. It was hard work. When we stopped to rest, we saw that the neighbors were starting their gardens too.

"Hello, Irma!" my mother called to Mrs. Crumerine.
Mrs. Crumerine was digging too. She was using a small
shovel, one that fit in her hand.

"Mommy," I asked, "why are we using such big
shovels? Mrs. Crumerine has a small one."

"Because our garden needs more digging," she said.

I helped my mother plant the seeds, and we dragged the hose to the garden.

"Hi, Linda! Hi, Mickey!" I called to the Fitzgeralds. They were sprinkling water on their garden with green watering cans.

"Mommy," I asked, "why are we using a hose? Linda and Mickey use watering cans."

"Because our garden needs more water," she said.

 STOP AND THINK

Conclusions What can you tell about the people in this neighborhood? Explain your answer.

TEKS 2.3C, 2.9B

Then my mother drew funny pictures on pieces of
paper, and I stuck them into the garden.

"Hello, Roseanne!" my mother called across the street
to Mrs. Angelhowe.

"Mommy," I asked, "why are we sticking these papers
in the garden? Mrs. Angelhowe has seed packages in her
garden."

"Because our garden is going to grow Chinese
vegetables," she told me. "These are the names of the
vegetables in Chinese, so I can tell which plants are
growing where."

One day I saw our garden growing. Little green
stems that looked like grass had popped out from the
ground.

"Our garden's growing!" I yelled. "Our garden's
growing!"

I rushed over to the neighbors' gardens to see if theirs
had grown. Their plants looked like little leaves.

"Mommy," I asked, "why do our plants look like
grass? The neighbors' plants look different."

"Because they are growing flowers," she said.

"Why can't we grow flowers?" I asked.

"These are better than flowers," she said.

Soon all the neighbors' gardens were blooming. Up
and down the street grew rainbows of flowers.

The wind always smelled sweet, and butterflies and bees flew everywhere. Everyone's garden was beautiful, except for ours.

Ours was all dark green and ugly.

"Why didn't we grow flowers?" I asked again.

"These are better than flowers," Mommy said again.

I looked, but saw only black-purple-green vines, fuzzy wrinkled leaves, prickly stems, and a few little yellow flowers.

"I don't think so," I said.

"You wait and see," Mommy said.

Before long, our vegetables grew. Some were big and lumpy. Some were thin and green and covered with bumps. Some were just plain icky yellow. They were ugly vegetables.

Sometimes I would go over to the neighbors' and look at their pretty gardens. They would show the poppies and peonies and petunias to me, and I would feel sad that our garden wasn't as nice.

One day my mother and I picked the vegetables from the garden. We filled a whole wheelbarrow full of them. We wheeled them to the kitchen. My mother washed them and took a big knife and started to chop them.

"Aie-yow!" she said when she cut them. She had to use all her muscles. The vegetables were hard and tough.

"This is sheau hwang gua (show hwang gwa)," Mommy said, handing me a bumpy, curled vegetable. She pointed at the other vegetables. "This is shiann tsay (shen zai). That's a torng hau (tung how)."

I went outside to play. While I was playing catch with Mickey, a magical aroma filled the air. I saw the neighbors standing on their porches with their eyes closed, smelling the sky. They took deep breaths of air, like they were trying to eat the smell.

The wind carried it up and down the street. Even
the bees and the butterflies seemed to smell the scent
in the breeze.

I smelled it too. It made me hungry, and it was coming from my house!

When I followed it to my house, my mother was putting a big bowl of soup on the table. The soup was yellow and red and green and pink.

"This is a special soup," Mommy said, and she smiled.

She gave me a small bowl full of it and I tasted it. It was so good! The flavors of the soup seemed to dance in my mouth and laugh all the way down to my stomach. I smiled.

"Do you like it?" Mommy asked me.

I nodded and held out my bowl for some more.

"It's made from our vegetables," she told me.

> **STOP AND THINK**
> **Author's Craft** What does the author write that tells how good the soup tastes?
> TEKS 2.3B

Then the doorbell rang, and we ran to open the door.
All our neighbors were standing at the door holding
flowers.

"We noticed you were cooking." Mr. Fitzgerald
laughed as he held out his flowers. "And we thought
maybe you might be interested in a trade!"

 **STOP AND THINK**
Analyze/Evaluate Would this
neighborhood be a good place to
live? Use details to tell why.
TEKS 2.3B

We laughed too, and my mother gave them each their own bowl of her special soup.

My mother told them what each vegetable was and how she grew it. She gave them the soup recipe and put some soup into jars for them to take home. I ate five bowls of soup.

It was the best dinner ever.

The next spring, when my mother was starting her garden, we planted some flowers next to the Chinese vegetables. Mrs. Crumerine, the Fitzgeralds, and the Angelhowes planted some Chinese vegetables next to their flowers.

Soon the whole neighborhood was growing Chinese vegetables in their gardens. Up and down the street, little green plants poked out of the ground. Some looked like leaves and some looked like grass, and when the flowers started blooming, you could smell soup in the air.

Your Turn

1. What happens after the girl tastes the soup?

   ⬭ She does not like the soup.

   ⬭ She holds out her bowl for more.

   ⬭ The neighbors' flowers start to grow.

2. 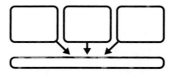 **TARGET SKILL** **Conclusions**

   Does Mommy like growing vegetables? Write your conclusion and the story clues in a chart. **TEKS** 2.9B

   ```
   ┌──┐ ┌──┐ ┌──┐
   └──┘ └──┘ └──┘
      ↘   ↓   ↙
   ┌────────────┐
   └────────────┘
   ```

3. **TARGET STRATEGY** **Analyze/Evaluate**

   What lesson does the girl learn in this story? Why is this an important lesson to learn?

4. **Oral Language** Use the Retelling Cards to tell what happens before and after the neighbors smell the soup. **TEKS** 2.6A, **ELPS** 4K

Retelling Cards

 TEKS 2.6A identify moral lessons in well-known tales; **2.9B** describe characters' traits/motivations/feelings; **ELPS 4K** employ analytical skills to demonstrate comprehension

They Really Are GIANT!

by Judy Williams

To some farmers, plain, ordinary-sized vegetables seem boring. These farmers think big. They like to grow the biggest vegetables ever.

World Record Breakers

Plants are always blooming in California. The scent of rich soil fills the air. Every year in Half Moon Bay, the town holds the World Championship Pumpkin Weigh-Off. The judges all nodded yes when they saw the 2007 winner. It weighed 1,524 pounds, more than a big horse!

Pumpkins aren't the only giant veggies though. Some farmers use their muscles and heavy shovels to dig up 30-pound beets and turnips. Although these giants look tough, they are tender and delicious to eat.

Thadd Starr won first prize at the Half Moon Bay contest for his super-sized pumpkin.

Home of the Giants

Alaska might be the home of giant veggies. More giant vegetables seem to grow there than any other place in the world. Long summer days and good soil make veggies grow and grow. You can see 98-pound cabbages at the Alaska State Fair in Palmer.

Seven-year-old Brenna Dinkel from Wasilla, Alaska, looks small next to this giant wrinkled leaf cabbage!

How Big Are They?

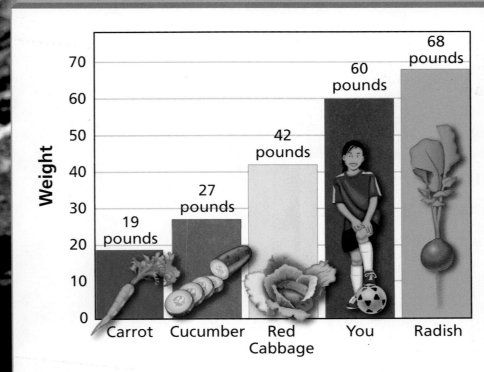

Weight

Vegetable	Weight
Carrot	19 pounds
Cucumber	27 pounds
Red Cabbage	42 pounds
You	60 pounds
Radish	68 pounds

Making Connections

 Text to Self TEKS RC-2(F)

Make a List List the steps that the characters take to plant and care for their vegetables in *The Ugly Vegetables*. Which step do you think is the most fun?

 Text to Text TEKS 2.19C

Compare Vegetables Would you rather grow ugly vegetables like those in *The Ugly Vegetables* or giant ones like those in "They Really Are Giant!"? Explain.

 Text to World TEKS 2.28A, ELPS 3E

Connect to Social Studies In *The Ugly Vegetables*, Mommy says she is growing Chinese vegetables. Find China on a map or globe. Talk with a partner about what you found. Listen carefully to what your partner says.

 TEKS **2.19C** write brief comments on texts; **2.28A** listen/ask clarifying questions; **RC-2(F)** make connections to experiences/texts/community; **ELPS** **3E** share information in cooperative learning interactions

Grammar

Proper Nouns **Proper nouns** are the special names of people, animals, places, or things. Proper nouns begin with **capital letters**.

Academic Language

proper nouns
capital letters

Nouns	Proper Nouns
neighbor	Roseanne Smith
pet	Fluffy
road	Main Street
state	Texas
country	China

Try This! **Write each sentence correctly. Remember to begin the proper nouns with capital letters.**

1 There are many gardens in centerville.

2 My friend molly bowen picked apples.

3 Our dog spot is digging up the roses!

Word Choice A proper noun names a special person, animal, place, or thing. A proper noun is one kind of exact noun. Use exact nouns in your writing to paint a picture in your reader's mind.

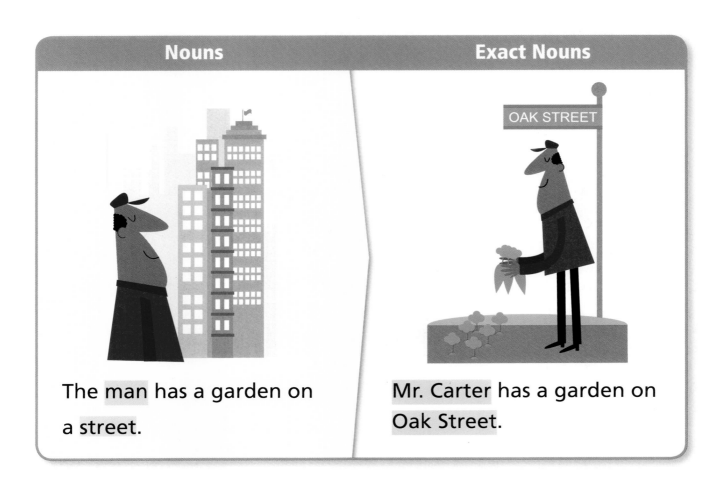

Nouns	Exact Nouns
The man has a garden on a street.	Mr. Carter has a garden on Oak Street.

Connect Grammar to Writing

When you revise your summary paragraph, look for nouns you can change to more exact nouns.

Write to Inform

☑ **Organization** A **summary** tells what happens in a story. It puts the events in the same order.

Kayla drafted a summary of the first part of *The Ugly Vegetables*. Later, she put the events in the right order.

Writing Traits Checklist

☑ **Idea**
Did my sentences all tie to the main idea?

☑ **Organization**
Did I tell things in the order in which they happened?

☑ **Sentence Fluency**
Are the words in my sentences in an order that makes sense?

☑ **Conventions**
Did I capitalize and punctuate my sentences correctly?

Revised Draft

A girl helps her mother start a garden. The girl keeps seeing things they're doing differently from their neighbors. To water the garden, she and her mother use a hose. The neighbors use watering cans. The neighbors are using smaller shovels.

My Summary

by Kayla Higgs

A girl helps her mother start a garden. The girl keeps seeing things they're doing differently from their neighbors. The neighbors are using smaller shovels. To water the garden, she and her mother use a hose. The neighbors use watering cans. She and her mother stick pictures in their garden. The girl asks why their garden is different from the neighbors' flower gardens. Her mother says the vegetables they are growing are better than flowers.

I moved sentences around to tell things in the order in which they happened.

Reading as a Writer

Why did Kayla move sentences? What can you move in your writing to put events in the right order?

225

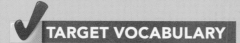
TARGET VOCABULARY

beware

damage

bend

flash

pounding

prevent

reach

equal

Vocabulary
Reader

Context
Cards

TEKS **2.5B** use context to determine meaning; **ELPS** **3D** speak using content-area vocabulary; **4C** develop/comprehend basic English vocabulary and structures

Vocabulary in Context

- **Read each Context Card.**

- **Talk about a picture. Use a different Vocabulary word from the one on the card.**

1
beware
Beware of dangerous weather when a storm siren sounds its warning.

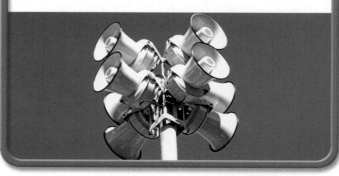

2
damage
Hail and strong winds can do a lot of harm. They can damage crops.

3 bend

High winds have caused the trunks of these trees to bend, or curve.

4 flash

The flash of lightning bolts lit up the dark night sky.

5 pounding

Pounding waves hit the beach hard in a storm.

6 prevent

Heavy snow may prevent, or stop, cars and trucks from traveling.

7 reach

In a flood, water can reach, or go as high as, rooftops.

8 equal

The height of the snow is equal to three feet.

Background

✔ TARGET VOCABULARY **Storm Warning** Beware! A flash of lightning or a boom of thunder means a storm is coming. Strong winds that bend big trees are another sign of a storm. Pounding hailstones can damage homes and cars. One way to prevent getting hurt in a storm is to pay attention to the sky. Clouds shaped like a funnel equal a tornado. You need to find a safe place before the storm can reach where you are.

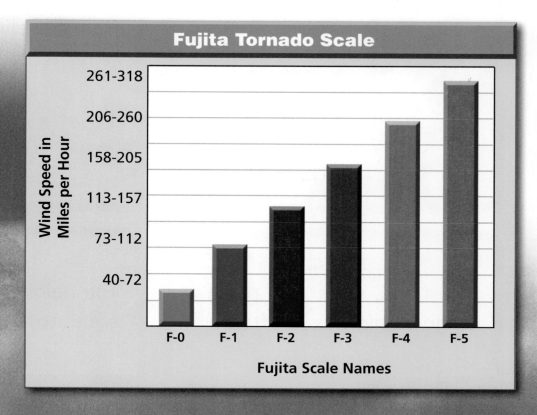

Fujita Tornado Scale

Wind Speed in Miles per Hour

261-318	
206-260	
158-205	
113-157	
73-112	
40-72	

F-0   F-1   F-2   F-3   F-4   F-5

Fujita Scale Names

This chart shows how scientists indicate the strength of a tornado.

228

TEKS **2.3B** ask questions/clarify/locate facts/details/support with evidence; **2.14A** identify main idea/distinguish from topic; **2.14B** locate facts in text; **RC-2(C)** monitor/adjust comprehension; **ELPS** **4D** use prereading supports to comprehend texts; **4I** employ reading skills to demonstrate comprehension

Comprehension

✓ TARGET SKILL Main Ideas and Details

Use the title to help you figure out the topic of *Super Storms*. Then, as you read, think about the main, or important, ideas about the different storms. Use a web like this to note details that tell about each main idea.

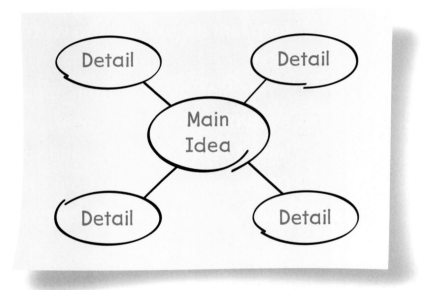

✓ TARGET STRATEGY Visualize

Use details about each main idea to help you visualize, or form a picture of, what the author is describing. The pictures you form will help you remember main ideas about different kinds of storms.

JOURNEYS DIGITAL Powered by DESTINATIONReading
Comprehension Activities: Lesson 8

229

TARGET VOCABULARY

beware	pounding
damage	prevent
bend	reach
flash	equal

TARGET SKILL

Main Ideas and Details Tell important ideas and details about a topic.

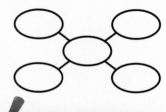

TARGET STRATEGY

Visualize Picture what is happening as you read.

GENRE
Informational text gives facts about a topic.

MEET THE AUTHOR

SEYMOUR SIMON

As a former science teacher, Seymour Simon loves to visit classrooms and talk with students. Those visits sometimes help him decide what to write about next.

Mr. Simon has written about everything from bats, bears, and bugs to snakes, sharks, and spiders. Of the more than 200 books he has written, *The Paper Airplane Book* is one of his favorites.

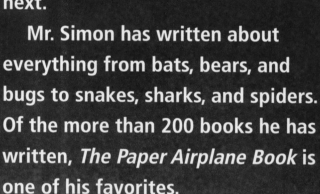

SUPER STORMS

by Seymour Simon

Essential Question

How do you know what a story is mostly about?

The air around us is always moving and changing. We call these changes weather. Storms are sudden, violent changes in weather.

Every second, hundreds of thunderstorms are born around the world. Thunderstorms are heavy rain showers. They can drop millions of gallons of water in just one minute.

During a thunderstorm, lightning bolts can shoot between clouds and the ground. Lightning can destroy a tree or a small house. It can also start fires in forests and grasslands.

Thunder is the sound lightning makes as it suddenly heats the air. You can tell how far away lightning is. Count the seconds between the flash of light and the sound of thunder. Five seconds equal one mile.

CtN

Hailstones are chunks of ice that are tossed up and down by the winds of some thunderstorms. Hail can be the size of a marble or larger than a baseball. Nearly 5,000 hailstorms strike the United States every year. They can destroy crops and damage buildings and cars.

Thunderstorms sometimes give birth to tornadoes. Inside a storm, a funnel-shaped cloud reaches downward. Winds inside a tornado can spin faster than 300 miles per hour. These winds can lift cars off the ground and rip houses apart.

✔ STOP AND THINK

Main Ideas and Details What is the main idea of this paragraph?

TEKS 2.14A

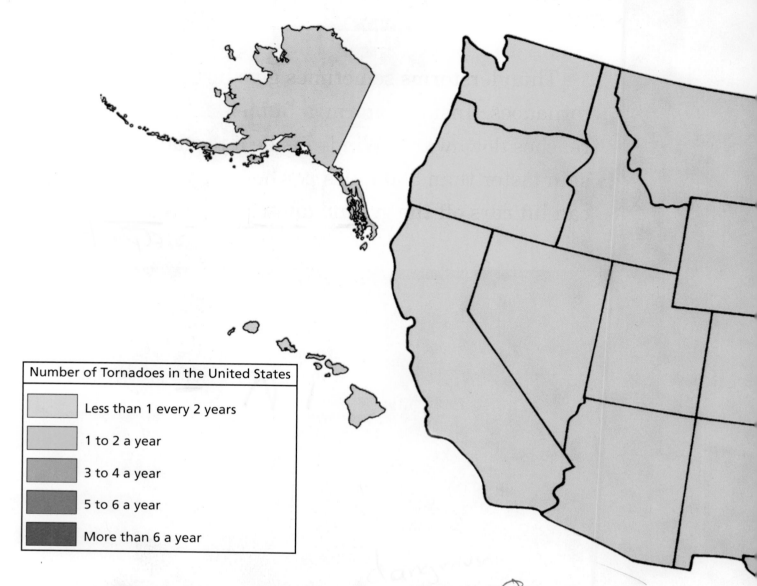

Number of Tornadoes in the United States

	Less than 1 every 2 years
	1 to 2 a year
	3 to 4 a year
	5 to 6 a year
	More than 6 a year

More than 1,000 tornadoes strike the United States each year. Most of them form during spring and summer.

Television and radio stations often give early alerts. A tornado watch means that one may strike during the next few hours. A warning means a tornado has been seen by people or on radar. During a tornado warning you should find shelter in a basement or closet.

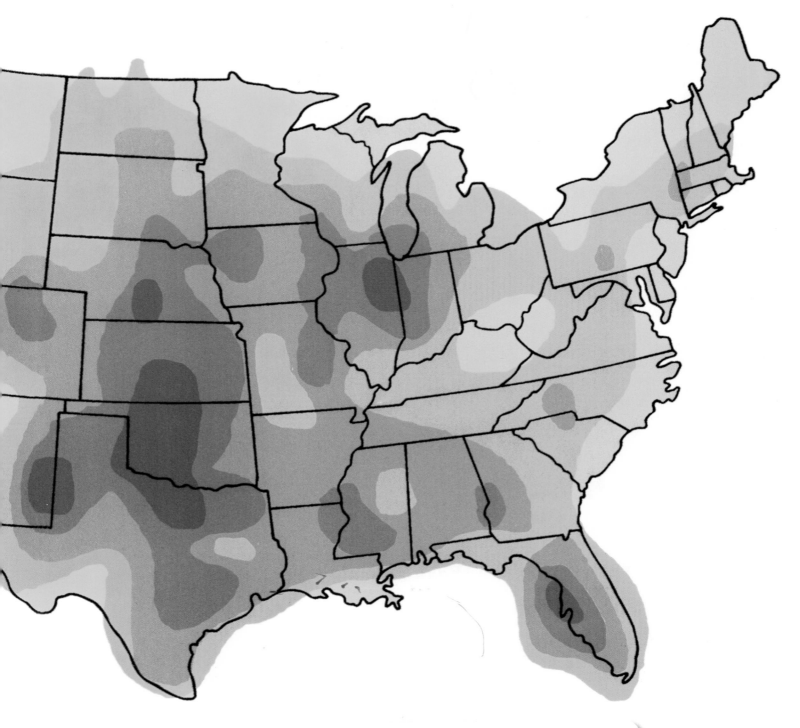

✔ STOP AND THINK
Visualize How do the colors on the map show where the greatest and the least danger is from tornadoes?
TEKS RC-2(C)

dangrous

Hurricanes are the deadliest storms in the world. They kill more people than all other storms combined. Hurricanes stretch for hundreds of miles. They have winds of between 74 and 200 miles per hour. *a*

The eye of a hurricane is the quiet center of the storm. Inside the eye, the wind stops blowing, the sun shines, and the sky is blue. But beware, the storm is not over yet.

center

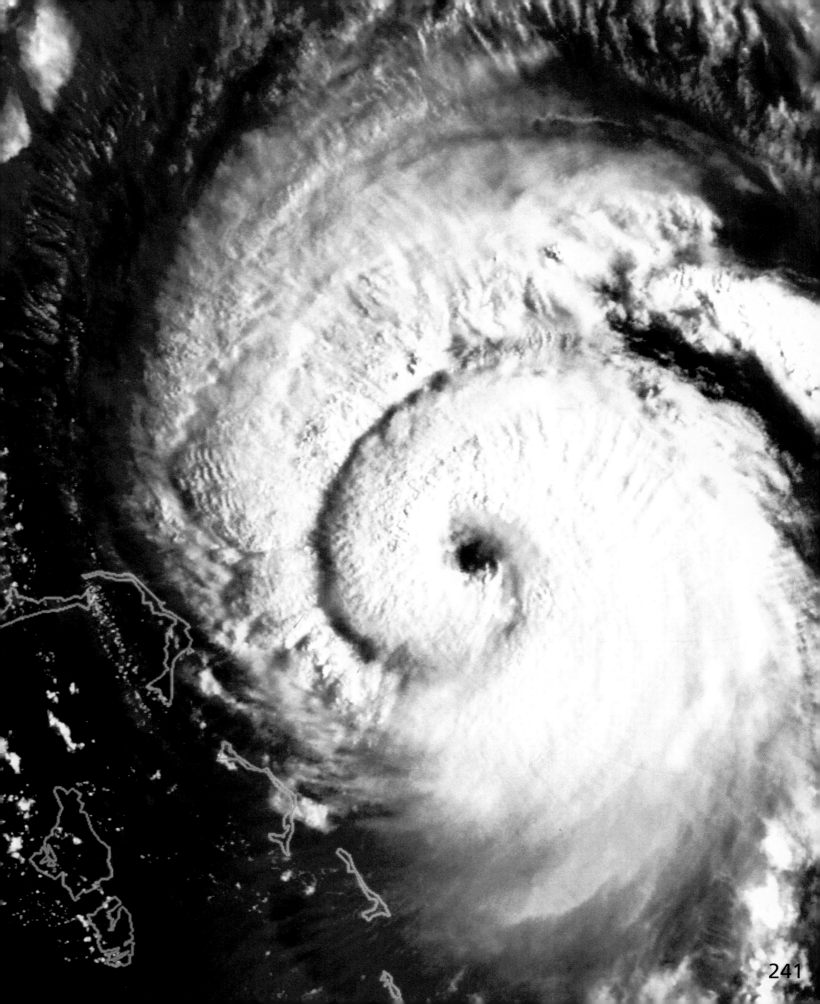

Hurricanes are born over warm ocean waters from early summer to mid-fall. When they finally reach land, their pounding waves wash away beaches, boats, and houses. Their howling winds bend and uproot trees and telephone poles. Their heavy rains cause floods.

Blizzards are huge snowstorms. They have winds of at least 35 miles per hour. Usually at least two inches of snow falls per hour. Temperatures are at 20 degrees or lower. Falling and blowing snow make it hard to see in a blizzard.

No one can prevent storms. But weather reports can predict and warn us when a storm may hit. The more prepared we are, the safer we will be when the next one strikes.

Use context to determine word meanings.

1. On page 244, the word <u>prevent</u> means to —

⬭ start

⬭ enjoy

⬭ stop

TEKS 2.5B

2. ✔ TARGET SKILL **Main Ideas and Details**
What main idea and details have you learned about blizzards? Use a web like this to answer. TEKS 2.14A

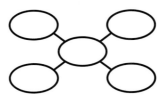

3. ✔ TARGET STRATEGY **Visualize**
Use text details to visualize a town hit by a blizzard.
Describe what you picture. ELPS 3H

4. Oral Language Tell about storms with a partner.
Ask a question if you don't understand something.
TEKS 2.28A, ELPS 3F, 4G

 TEKS **2.5B** use context to determine meaning; **2.14A** identify main idea/distinguish from topic; **2.28A** listen/ask clarifying questions; **ELPS** **3F** ask/give information in various contexts; **3H** narrate/describe/explain with detail; **4G** demonstrate comprehension through shared reading/retelling/responding/note-taking

✓ TARGET VOCABULARY

beware	pounding
damage	prevent
bend	reach
flash	equal

GENRE

Poetry uses the sound of words to show pictures and feelings.

TEXT FOCUS

Repetition is the same words used more than once.

Weather Poems

Many poets write poems about the weather. They might write about a flash of lightning or the way winds bend flowers.

The three poems you will read next are about the weather. Listen to the words that repeat in the poem "Night Drumming for Rain." Does it remind you of pounding raindrops?

Night Drumming for Rain

hi-iya nai-ho-o
earth rumbling
earth rumbling
our basket drum sounding
earth rumbling
everywhere humming
everywhere raining

Pima

Rain

Windy winter rain . . .
    my silly big
    umbrella
tries walking backward

by Shisei-Jo
Translated from Japanese
by Peter Beilenson

Morning Sun

warming up
my bed
in the morning

the Sun
calls me
through the window

"wake up
get up
come on out"

by Francisco X. Alarcón

Write a Weather Poem

Write your own weather poem. You might describe how hot, sunny days equal summer fun. You might warn friends to beware of a storm that is about to reach them or damage a special place. You might even write a funny poem on how to prevent a storm!

Making Connections

TEKS 2.30

Text to Self

Make a Plan Choose one type of storm from *Super Storms*. With the class, discuss what you would do to stay safe in that kind of weather. Speak only when it is your turn.

Text to Text

Connect to Science Think about the weather in *Super Storms* and "Weather Poems." Draw pictures of the two you found most interesting. Write a caption for each picture.

Tornadoes have strong winds that twirl.

Text to World

TEKS RC(2)-F

Observe Local Weather What kinds of weather do you get where you live? List each type. Compare your list with a partner's.

 TEKS **2.30** follow discussion rules; **RC(2)-F** make connections to experiences/texts/community

Grammar

What Is a Verb? A **verb** names an action that someone or something does or did. A verb is found in the action part, or **predicate**, of a sentence.

Academic Language

verb

predicate

Verbs in Sentences

Rain falls.

Strong winds blow.

The storm destroyed homes.

The tornado bent many trees.

 **Work with a partner. Read the sentences aloud. Name the verb in each sentence.**

1. I learned about storms.

2. We stay indoors.

3. Tornadoes form in summer.

4. The thunder scared my cat.

Word Choice When you write, use exact verbs. They make your sentences come alive and tell your reader exactly what is happening.

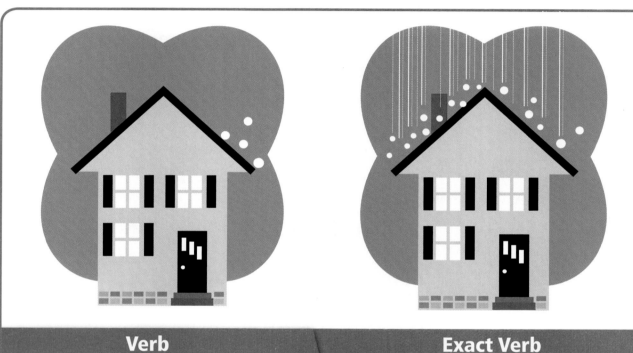

Verb	Exact Verb
The hail **touched** the roof.	The hail **pounded** the roof.
The hail **hurt** the roof	The hail **damaged** the roof.

Connect Grammar to Writing

When you revise your writing, look for verbs that you can change to more exact verbs.

Write to Inform

☑ **Voice** When you write an **informational paragraph**, remember to use your own words. Do not copy words that were written by someone else.

Greg drafted a paragraph about thunderstorms. He used facts from *Super Storms*. Later, he revised some sentences to be in his own words.

Writing Traits Checklist

☑ **Ideas**
Did I use facts instead of opinions?

☑ **Voice**
Did I use my own words?

☑ **Sentence Fluency**
Did I get rid of short, choppy sentences?

☑ **Conventions**
Did I write neatly and leave margins?

Revised Draft

Thunderstorms bring lots of
Millions of gallons of rain
rain. ~~They can drop millions of~~
can fall in one minute.
~~gallons of water in just one~~

~~minute.~~ Lightning bolts destroy

trees and houses.
Lightning can also start fires in
~~They can also start fires in~~
trees or grass!
~~forests and grasslands.~~

Thunderstorms

by Greg Popov

Thunderstorms bring lots of rain. Millions of gallons of rain can fall in one minute. Lightning bolts destroy trees and houses. Lightning can also start fires in trees or grass! People can tell how close lightning is by counting the seconds between lightning and the sound of thunder. For every five seconds you count, the lightning is one mile away.

I made sure I used my own words to tell facts.

Reading as a Writer

How did Greg tell facts in his own way? What parts of your paragraph can you retell in your own words?

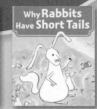

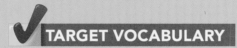

TARGET VOCABULARY

tunnel

curled

height

direction

toward

healed

brag

tease

Vocabulary Reader   Context Cards

TEKS 2.5B use context to determine meaning; **ELPS** 1F use accessible language to learn new language

Vocabulary in Context

- Read each **Context Card**.

- Ask a question that uses one of the Vocabulary words.

1
tunnel
A chipmunk knows how to dig a tunnel, which is a passage underground.

2
curled
This fox is curled up around its warm, bushy tail.

3 height

An eagle builds its nest at an amazing height. It is at the top of a tall tree.

4 direction

An owl can turn its head in any direction. It can look all around.

5 toward

These bear cubs run toward their mother so she can protect them.

6 healed

This pangolin will go back to the forest when it is well, or healed.

7 brag

These antlers are something to brag about! They are huge.

8 tease

Never tease, or bother, wild animals. Always respect them.

Background

TARGET VOCABULARY **Folktales** A folktale is a story that people have been telling for many years. Some folktale characters brag about their strength or height. That gets them into trouble. Some characters tease others. That causes trouble, too. A folktale can explain why Bear's injured tail healed as it did or why Squirrel's tail is curled toward its back. It can tell why Mole hid in a tunnel or why certain travelers went in the direction of a village.

An American Indian tale tells how Coyote brought people fire.

256

TEKS 2.3C establish purpose/monitor comprehension; 2.9B describe characters' traits/motivations/feelings; RC-2(C) monitor/adjust comprehension; ELPS 4I employ reading skills to demonstrate comprehension

Comprehension

✔ TARGET SKILL Understanding Characters

In *How Chipmunk Got His Stripes,* Bear and Brown Squirrel speak and act like people. Use story clues and what you know to figure out why the characters act that way. List story clues and your ideas on a chart like this one.

Words	Actions	What I Know

✔ TARGET STRATEGY Summarize

As you read, summarize, or express in your own words, why Bear and Brown Squirrel act as they do. Summarizing will help you better understand the story. If you do not understand, slowly reread the text.

Main Selection

TARGET VOCABULARY

tunnel	toward
curled	healed
height	brag
direction	tease

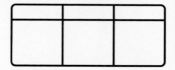
Understanding Characters Tell more about characters.

Summarize Stop to tell important events as you read.

GENRE
A **folktale** is a story that is often told by people of a country.

MEET THE AUTHORS

Joseph Bruchac and James Bruchac

As a boy, Joseph Bruchac listened to his grandfather tell stories of their Native American heritage. Joseph passed these stories down to his son, James. Now this father-and-son team writes books together, such as *Raccoon's Last Race.*

MEET THE ILLUSTRATORS

Jose Aruego and Ariane Dewey

These two artists make a great team. When they are working on a book, Jose Aruego first draws the lines for the characters, using pen and ink. Then Ariane Dewey paints the colors. In this way, they have illustrated more than 60 books.

How Chipmunk Got His Stripes

by Joseph Bruchac and James Bruchac
pictures by Jose Aruego and Ariane Dewey

Essential Question

What can you learn from the way a character acts?

One autumn day long ago, Bear was out walking.
As he walked, he began to brag:

"I am Bear. I am the biggest
of all the animals. Yes, I am!
I am Bear. I am the strongest
of all the animals. Yes, I am!
I am Bear. I am the loudest
of all the animals. Yes, I am!
I am Bear, I am Bear.
I can do anything. Yes, I can!"

As soon as Bear said those words, a little voice spoke up from the ground.

"Can you really do anything?"

Bear looked down. He saw a little brown squirrel, standing on his hind legs.

"Can you really do anything?" Brown Squirrel asked again.

Bear stood up very tall. "I am Bear. I can do anything. Yes, I can!"

"Can you tell the sun not to rise tomorrow morning?" Brown Squirrel asked.

"I have never tried that before. But I am Bear. I can do that. Yes, I can!"

> ✔ **STOP AND THINK**
> **Understanding Characters** What tells you that Bear thinks he is wonderful?
> **TEKS** 2.3B, 2.9B

Bear turned west to face the sun. It was the time when the sun always goes down. Bear stood up to his full height and spoke in a loud voice.

"SUN, DO NOT COME UP TOMORROW."

At his words, the sun began to disappear behind the hills.

"You see?" Bear said. "Sun is afraid of me. He is running away."

"But will the sun come up tomorrow?" Brown Squirrel asked.

"No," Bear answered. "The sun will not come up!"

Then Bear turned to face east, the direction where the sun always used to come up. He sat down. Little Brown Squirrel sat down beside him. All that night, they did not sleep. All that night, Bear kept saying these words:

"The sun will not come up, hummph!
The sun will not come up, hummph!"

But as the night went on, little Brown Squirrel began to say something, too. He said these words:

"The sun is going to rise, oooh!
The sun is going to rise, oooh!"

All through the night, they sat there. One by one, other animals gathered around them. Fox and Wolf, Deer and Moose, Rabbit and Porcupine, Hawk and Owl, Otter and Beaver, Frog and Turtle, and even the little mice came. They wanted to see who would be right, Bear or Brown Squirrel. This is what the other animals heard:

"The sun will not come up, hummph!"
"The sun is going to rise, oooh!"
"The sun will not come up, hummph!"
"The sun is going to rise, oooh!"

STOP AND THINK
Author's Craft Why does the author keep repeating Bear's sentence and little Brown Squirrel's sentence?

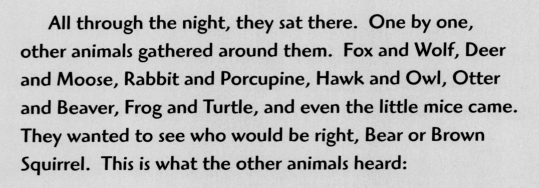

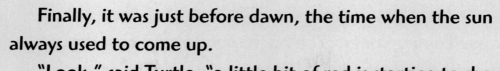

Finally, it was just before dawn, the time when the sun always used to come up.

"Look," said Turtle, "a little bit of red is starting to show."

"Yes," said Owl. "I believe the sun will rise today."

Bear only chanted louder:

"The sun will not come up, hummph!"

But right next to him, little Brown Squirrel piped up:

"The sun is going to rise, oooh!"

And the sun came up. The birds sang their welcoming songs. The bright light of the new day spread over the land. Everyone was happy except for one animal. That animal was Bear. He sat there with his head down and a grumpy look on his face.

The happiest animal of all was little Brown Squirrel. "The sun came up," he chirped. "The sun came up, the sun came up, the sun came up."

Brown Squirrel was so happy, he forgot what his wise old grandmother had told him when he was very young.

"Brown Squirrel," his grandmother had said, "it is good to be right about something. But when someone else is wrong, it is not a good idea to tease him."

Now little Brown Squirrel began to tease Bear.

"Bear is foolish, the sun came up.
Bear is silly, the sun came up.
Bear is stupid, the sun—"

267

WHOMP!

Bear's big paw came down on little Brown Squirrel, pinning him to the ground. Bear leaned over and opened his huge mouth.

"Yes," Bear growled. "The sun did come up. Yes, I do look foolish. But you will not live to see another sunrise. You will not ever tease anyone else again, because I, Bear, am going to eat you."

Brown Squirrel thought fast. "You are right to eat me," he said. "I was wrong to tease you. I would like to say I am sorry before you eat me. But you are pressing down on me so hard that I cannot say anything. I cannot say anything at all. I cannot even breathe. If you would lift up your paw just a little bit, then I could take a deep breath and apologize before you eat me."

"That is a good idea," Bear said. "I would like to hear you apologize before I eat you."

So Bear lifted up his paw. But instead of apologizing, Brown Squirrel ran. He ran as fast as he could toward the pile of stones where he had his home. He had a tunnel under those stones and a nice warm burrow underground. Little Brown Squirrel's grandmother stood there in the door waiting for him.

"Hurry, Brown Squirrel," she called. "Hurry, hurry!"

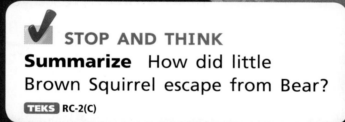

STOP AND THINK

Summarize How did little Brown Squirrel escape from Bear?

TEKS RC-2(C)

Little Brown Squirrel dove for the door to his home. But Bear was faster than he looked. He grabbed for little Brown Squirrel with his big paw. Bear's long, sharp claws scratched Brown Squirrel's back from the top of his head to the tip of his tail.

But Brown Squirrel got away. Deep down in his burrow, where Bear couldn't get him, Brown Squirrel curled up next to his grandmother and slept all winter while those scratches on his back healed.

When spring came again, little Brown Squirrel came out of his hole and looked at himself. There were long pale stripes all the way down his back where Bear had scratched him. He was Brown Squirrel no longer. He was now Chipmunk, the striped one.

That is how Chipmunk got his stripes. Ever since then, Chipmunk has been the first animal to get up every morning. As the sun rises, he scoots to the top of the tallest tree to sing his song:

"The sun came up,
the sun came up,
the sun came up,
the sun came up!"

And ever since then, Bear has been the last animal to get up. He doesn't like to hear Chipmunk's song. It reminds him—as it reminds us all—that no one, not even Bear, can do everything.

Your Turn

1. What is this story mostly about?

- ⬭ How Chipmunk learns a lesson
- ⬭ How forest animals work together
- ⬭ How Bear learns a lesson

2. 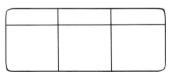 **TARGET SKILL** **Understanding Characters**

Will Chipmunk act the same way next time he hears an animal brag? Use a chart to answer. **TEKS 2.9B**

3. **TARGET STRATEGY** **Summarize**

Summarize how Chipmunk gets his stripes.
TEKS RC-2(E), **ELPS** 4I

4. Oral Language Use the Retelling Cards to tell what happens to Brown Squirrel after the sun comes up. **TEKS** RC-2(E)

Retelling Cards

 TEKS **2.9B** describe characters' traits/motivations/feelings; **RC-2(E)** retell important story events; **ELPS 4I** employ reading skills to demonstrate comprehension

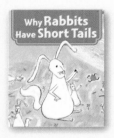

Why Rabbits Have Short Tails

✔ **TARGET VOCABULARY**

tunnel	toward
curled	healed
height	brag
direction	tease

GENRE
Traditional tales are stories that have been told for many years.

TEXT FOCUS
A **folktale** is a story that is passed down to explain or entertain.

Why Rabbits Have Short Tails

adapted by Gina Sabella

Once Rabbit had a long, beautiful tail. It curled over his back like a furry fan. Rabbit was taking his family on a trip.

"We have to travel in the direction of the stream," Rabbit said. "When we see the hill with the tallest height, we should head toward it."

When they spotted the tallest hill, Rabbit saw that they would have to swim across the stream.

Rabbit liked to brag. He told everyone how clever he was. He did not tell anyone that he could not swim. He did not want anyone to tease him.

Rabbit saw a turtle crawling out of a tunnel. Ten tiny turtles followed behind.

"You have a large family," Rabbit said.

"Yes," Turtle replied. "My family is the biggest in the woods."

"I'm not sure," Rabbit answered. "My family might be bigger."

"Line up your children across the stream," Rabbit said. "Then I can see who has a bigger family." Soon the turtles were lined up. Rabbit and his family jumped on their backs and skipped across the stream.

Turtle was not happy. He tried to grab Rabbit by the tail. But Rabbit's tail snapped off and he hopped away.

Even after it healed, Rabbit's tail never grew long and beautiful again.

Making Connections

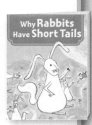

 Text to Self   TEKS RC-(2)F

Act Out a Lesson The characters in the stories you just read all learn a lesson. Act out for a partner a lesson you have learned. Have your partner guess what you learned.

 Text to Text   TEKS 2.6B, ELPS 4I

Compare Story Structure How are the characters, settings, and events in the two selections you just read the same and different? Write a few sentences to explain.

 Text to World

Explore Traditional Tales Are *How Chipmunk Got His Stripes* and *Why Rabbits Have Short Tails* made-up stories or true stories? Share your ideas with the class.

 TEKS **2.6B** compare folktale variants; **RC-(2)F** make connections to experiences/texts/community; **ELPS 4I** employ reading skills to demonstrate comprehension

Grammar

Verbs in the Present A **verb** in the **present** names an action that is happening now. Add -s or -es to this kind of verb when it tells about a singular noun. Do not add -s or -es when the verb tells about a plural noun.

Academic Language

verb

present

Verbs After Singular Nouns	Verbs After Plural Nouns
The bear sleeps.	Two bears sleep.
The animal runs.	Many animals run.
The chipmunk rushes.	Some chipmunks rush.

Try This! **Choose the correct verb to complete each sentence. Then write the sentence correctly.**

❶ The squirrel (learn, learns) a lesson.

❷ Bears (scratch, scratches)!

❸ The animal (hide, hides) in a hole.

❹ Days (pass, passes) before the animal comes out.

Sentence Fluency To make your writing smoother, join two short sentences with the same subject. Write **and** between the two predicates to make one longer sentence.

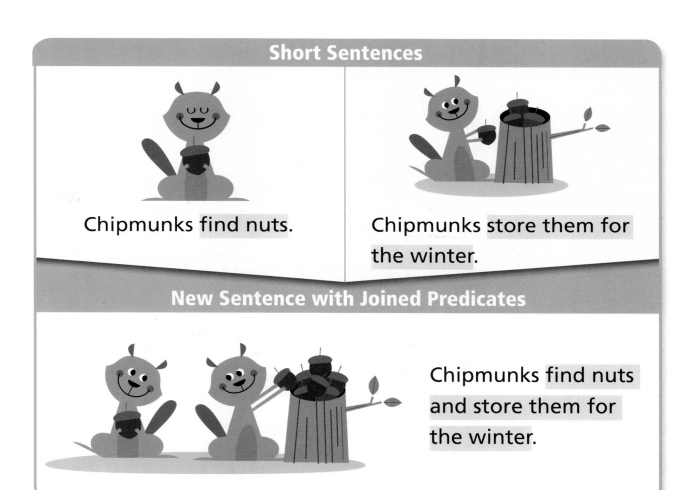

Short Sentences

Chipmunks find nuts.

Chipmunks store them for the winter.

New Sentence with Joined Predicates

Chipmunks find nuts and store them for the winter.

Connect Grammar to Writing

When you revise your instructions next week, try joining two sentences that have the same subject.

Reading-Writing Workshop: Prewrite

Write to Inform

✅ **Ideas** Before you write **instructions**, think about the important steps. What does your reader need to know to do this project?

When Alexa planned instructions for making a birdfeeder, she listed important materials and steps. Then she numbered the steps in order in a chart.

Writing Process Checklist

▶ **Prewrite**

✅ **Did I think about my audience and purpose?**

✅ **Did I choose a topic I know well?**

✅ **Did I include all the important steps?**

✅ **Are my steps in the correct order?**

Draft

Revise

Edit

Publish and Share

Exploring a Topic

Things You Need

pinecone

peanut butter

birdseed

spoon

∧paper plate

∧string

Steps

2 spread peanut butter on pinecone

4 hang on tree

3 roll in birdseed

1 ∧tie string to pinecone

1. Tie a piece of string to a pinecone.

2. Cover the pinecone with peanut butter.

3. Roll the pinecone in birdseed.

4. Hang the birdfeeder in a tree.

When I organized my instructions, I made sure I had all the important steps.

Reading as a Writer

What helpful steps did Alexa add? Where can you add important steps to your own chart?

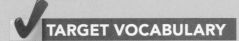
TARGET VOCABULARY

millions

choices

drift

simple

weaker

wrapped

disgusting

decide

Vocabulary Reader

Context Cards

TEKS 2.5B use context to determine meaning; **ELPS** 1E internalize new basic/ academic language; 4C develop/comprehend basic English vocabulary and structures

Vocabulary in Context

- **Read each Context Card.**

- **Tell a story about two pictures, using the Vocabulary words.**

1 millions

It looks like this shark has millions of teeth, but it really only has a few dozen.

2 choices

Visitors at the aquarium have many choices of things to see.

3 drift

This clever otter will not drift, or float, away.

4 simple

Dolphins make jumping out of the ocean look simple and easy.

5 weaker

One of these crab claws is weaker than the other. It is not very strong.

6 wrapped

The octopus wrapped its strong tentacles around its prey.

7 disgusting

Yuck! The litter around the trash can smells disgusting!

8 decide

Is this a starfish or a crab? You decide.

Background

Ocean Life Millions of animals live in the oceans. Jellyfish are very simple ocean animals. Stronger animals eat weaker animals. Once an octopus gets its legs wrapped around a clam, the clam will be its lunch. Blue whales eat tiny krill that drift by. Weaker animals have a few choices for protection. Squid squirt clouds of disgusting ink in which they hide. Once a jellyfish stings a turtle, the turtle will decide the jellyfish is not good to eat.

Oceans of the World

jellyfish

clam

octopus

squid

blue whale

Comprehension

✔ **TARGET SKILL** **Fact and Opinion**

Jellies contains many facts about jellyfish and some opinions. When you read, you must figure out which sentences give facts and which sentences state what the author feels or thinks. A chart like this can help.

Fact	Opinion

✔ **TARGET STRATEGY** **Monitor/Clarify**

As you read, stop to make sure you understand the story details. Readers monitor and clarify, or make sure they understand what they are reading, in order to make sense of new ideas and information. Your chart can help you.

Main Selection

THE LIFE OF JELLYFISH
Twig C. George

TARGET VOCABULARY

millions	weaker
choices	wrapped
drift	disgusting
simple	decide

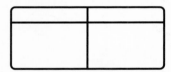
TARGET SKILL

Fact and Opinion Tell if an idea can be proved or is a feeling.

TARGET STRATEGY

Monitor/Clarify Find ways to figure out what doesn't make sense.

GENRE

Informational text gives facts about a topic.

MEET THE AUTHOR

Twig C. George

Twig C. George's love of nature began while she was growing up around her mom, writer Jean Craighead George. The George household had many unusual pets, including tarantulas, sea gulls, crows, and a screech owl that liked to take showers. Twig George raises her own children around nature, too.

Jellies
THE LIFE OF JELLYFISH

by Twig C. George

If you were a jellyfish you would have two choices—to go up or to go down. That's it. Two. You would not have a brain, so you could not decide what to have for breakfast or where to go for lunch.

Mangrove jellyfish

An unnamed jellyfish

The ocean currents would carry you along from place to place. In this way you could travel hundreds of miles. Food might pass by you and get caught in your tentacles. Or not.

Rhizostone
jellyfish

Sea turtles, dolphins, and whale sharks would try to eat you.

You wouldn't worry about it because you couldn't.

You would just float on.

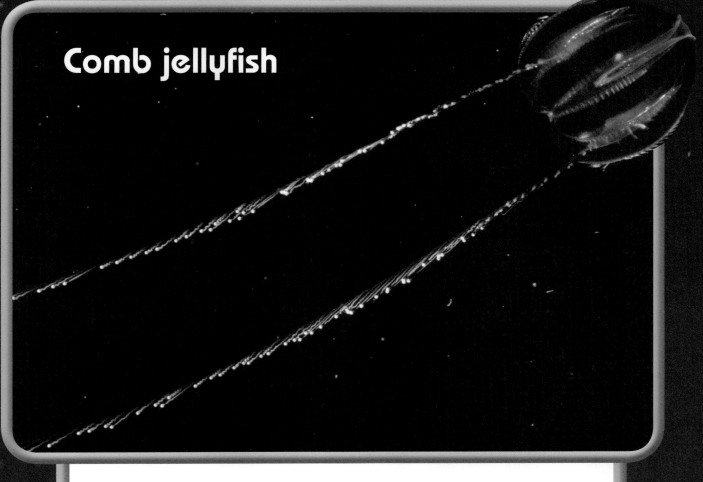

Comb jellyfish

You would protect yourself with millions of tiny, mechanical cells that, when touched by another animal, release a chemical and sting. Like a bow and arrow. You would not know if you were stinging a friend or an enemy. You would not even know what a friend or an enemy was!

Jellyfish sting for protection and to catch food. That's all. They don't hunt and they can't chase. They just bump and sting. Bump and sting.

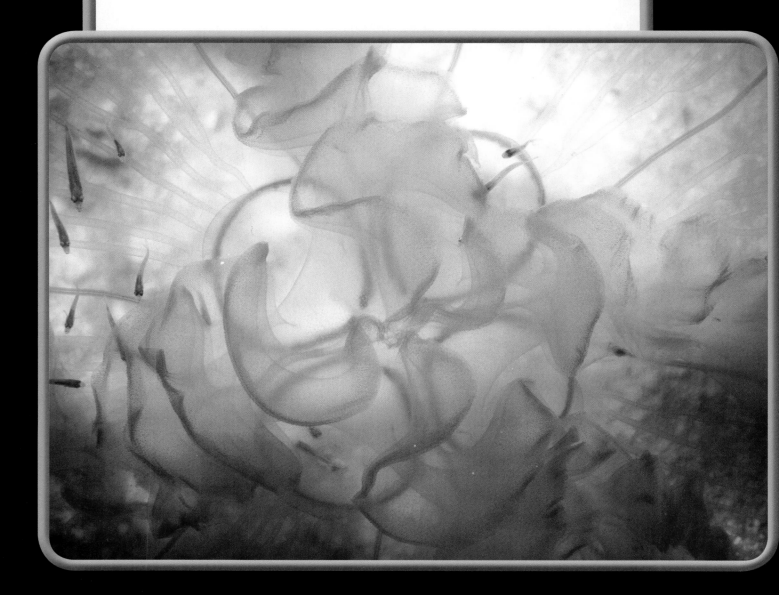

Little fish swim in and out of the dome of this moon jellyfish.

Some jellyfish sting gently. Some jellyfish have a sting so powerful that they are more dangerous than a cobra. These are the Australian box jellies.

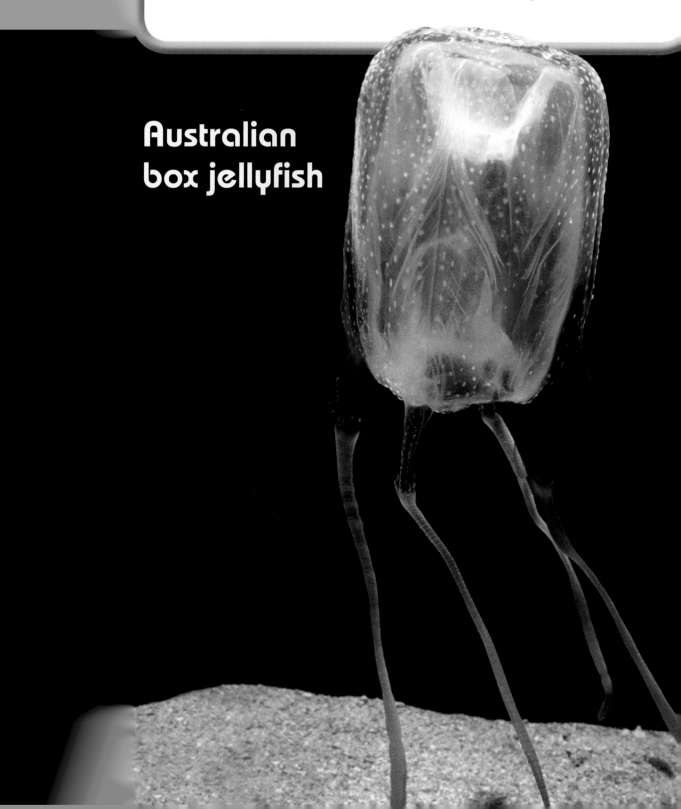

Australian
box jellyfish

Thimble jellyfish

Jellyfish are so simple that they look like plastic trash floating in the sea. When an animal eats a jellyfish it stays healthy and strong. When an animal eats plastic it gets weaker and weaker and eventually dies.

Upside-down jellyfish

Some jellyfish lie on the shallow bottom in clear, warm seas and grow their own food. These are called upside-down jellyfish. Once they have eaten small bits of algae, just once, they can grow more inside their bodies by sitting in the sun. They are their own greenhouses and grocery stores all wrapped up in one.

 STOP AND THINK
Monitor/Clarify What do you need to know to understand how upside-down jellyfish get food?
TEKS 2.3B

Portuguese man-of-war

To be a jellyfish you need to be shaped like a bell, with at least one mouth, and tentacles. Many animals called jellyfish are really something else. The Portuguese man-of-war is not a real jellyfish. It has an air-filled bubble instead of a water-filled bell.

Jellyfish are almost all water and a little protein. They look slimy and disgusting when they wash up on the beach.

Moon
jellyfish

✔ STOP AND THINK
Fact and Opinion What is one fact the author gives?
TEKS 2.3B

West Coast sea nettle

In the sea, jellyfish are beautiful. There are jellyfish as big as basketballs with long red tentacles, called West Coast sea nettles.

There are tiny, elegant jellyfish that look like a blizzard of snowflakes.

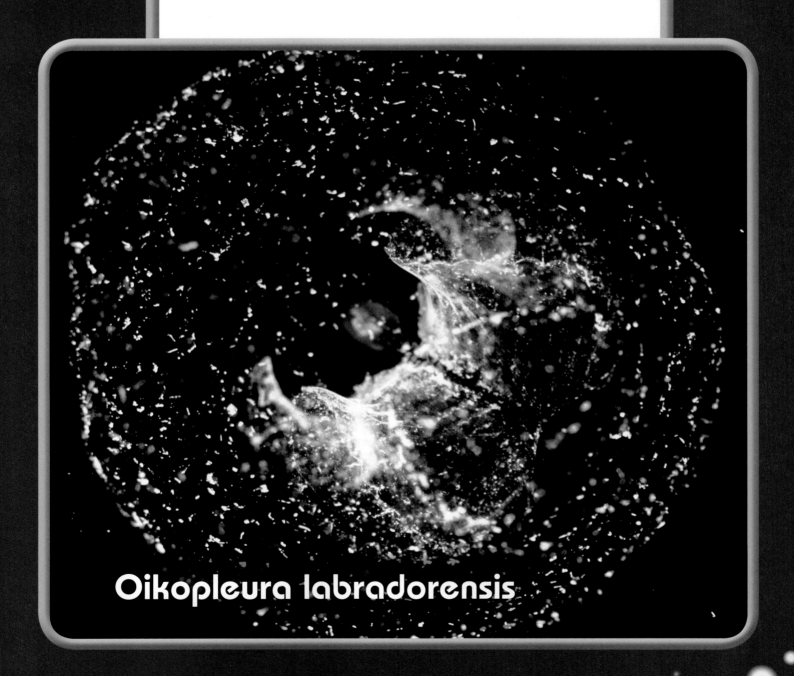

Oikopleura labradorensis

Arctic lion's mane jellyfish

There are jellyfish that grow so big that they are as long as a blue whale. They are called Arctic lion's mane jellyfish. They pulse and drift. They eat and reproduce. They live and die. All without a brain or a heart.

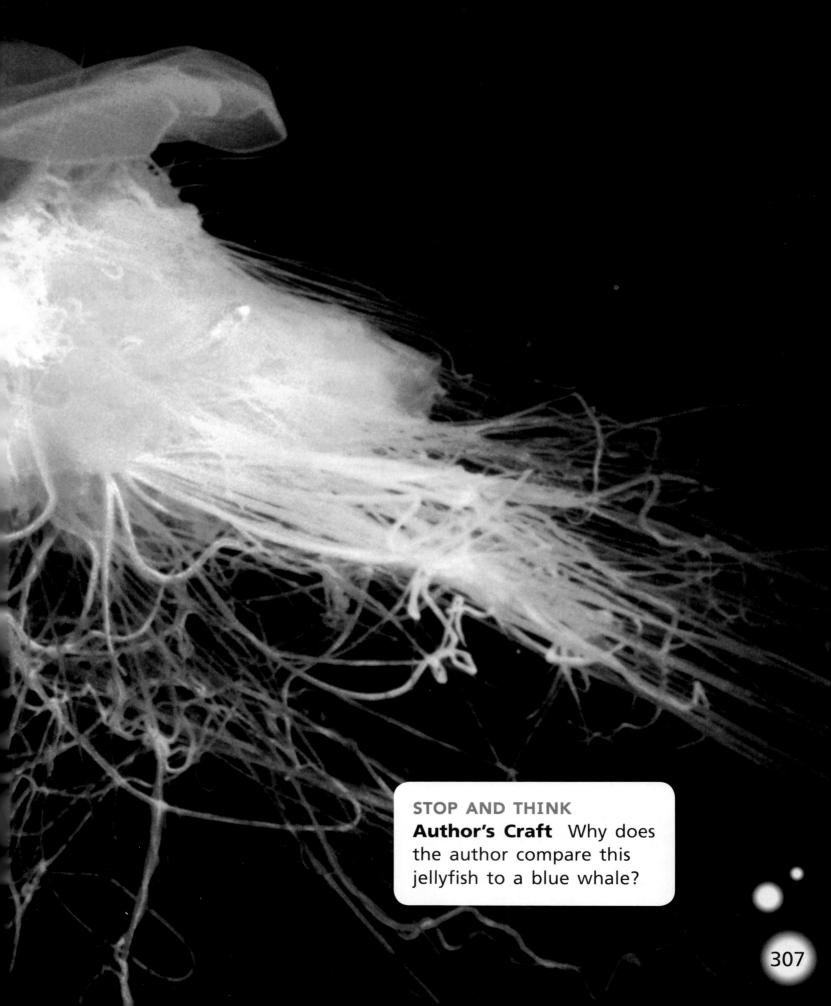

STOP AND THINK
Author's Craft Why does the author compare this jellyfish to a blue whale?

Golden Mastigias jellyfish

Someday you might be very lucky and see an ocean full of jellyfish. And, since you have a brain and a heart, you would know you were seeing something unforgettable.

Your Turn

1. On page 306, the word <u>drift</u> means to —

   ⬭ smile

   ⬭ jump

   ⬭ float

2. 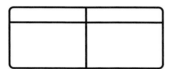 **TARGET SKILL** **Fact and Opinion**

   Write two interesting facts you learned about jellyfish.
   Then write your opinion about each fact. **TEKS** 2.3B, **ELPS** 4K

3. **TARGET STRATEGY** **Monitor/Clarify**

   How can the text on page 302 help you find out if the
   Portuguese man-of-war is a real jellyfish? **TEKS** 2.3B, 2.3C

4. **Oral Language** Use the Retelling Cards to
   tell what life would be like if you were a
   jellyfish. **ELPS** 3F

   Retelling Cards

 TEKS 2.3B ask questions/clarify/locate facts/details/support with evidence; **2.3C** establish purpose/monitor comprehension;
ELPS 3F ask/give information in various contexts; **4K** employ analytical skills to demonstrate comprehension

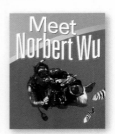

✔ TARGET VOCABULARY

millions	weaker
choices	wrapped
drift	disgusting
simple	decide

GENRE

Informational text gives facts about a topic. This is a social studies text.

TEXT FOCUS

A **diagram** is a drawing that shows how something works.

Meet Norbert Wu

A Day on the Job

When Norbert Wu goes to work, he grabs his flippers! Why? Mr. Wu works underwater. Millions of creatures live in the water. Wu's job is to take photos of them.

Choices to Make, Places to Go

Mr. Wu's job is not simple. He has to make a lot of choices. He must decide where to dive. He has to decide what camera to use. Some people might think it would be disgusting to be wet all the time.

Not Mr. Wu. He thinks his job is fun. He lives in California, but sometimes he travels. He has taken photos of Antarctic sea spiders. He has taken photos of Indonesian frogfish. He has seen sea cucumbers drift along the ocean floor and octopuses with their arms wrapped around their prey.

Dressed for Work

Wu uses special cameras to get the best photos. Check out what he wears to work!

Air Tank
This air tank holds the oxygen that Wu breathes.

Flippers
Feet are weaker than fins for swimming. Wu wears flippers so he can swim better.

Camera
Wu's camera is specially made so he can use it underwater.

Making Connections

TEKS RC-2(F)

Text to Self

Think About Jobs Would you rather write about ocean animals or take pictures of them? Explain using examples from the selections.

ELPS 4K

Text to Text

Compare Captions Choose one photo caption from *Jellies* and one from "Meet Norbert Wu." Tell your partner how captions can be alike and different.

TEKS 2.3B, 2.24B

Text to World

Connect to Science Choose an ocean animal you read about. Use other texts, such as magazine articles and encyclopedias to locate facts about that animal. Clarify the information you find in the other texts by asking questions.

Facts About Sharks

 TEKS **2.3B** ask questions/clarify/locate facts/details/support with evidence; **2.24B** determine relevant information sources; **RC-2(F)** make connections to experiences/texts/community; **ELPS 4K** employ analytical skills to demonstrate comprehension

Grammar

Verbs in the Present, Past, and Future Some **verbs** name actions that are happening now. Some verbs name actions that happened before, or in the **past**. Other verbs name actions that will happen later, or in the **future**.

Academic Language

verbs

past

future

Present	Past	Future
The jellies float.	The jellies floated.	The jellies will float.
We watch them.	We watched them.	We will watch them.

Turn and Talk **Work with a partner. Read the sentences aloud. Tell whether the action is happening in the present, in the past, or in the future.**

1 I like ocean animals.

2 Shelley enjoyed the waves.

3 The jellies swim all around.

4 We will visit the zoo tomorrow.

Sentence Fluency When you write, make sure your verbs tell about the same time. Your writing will be easier to understand.

Incorrect	Correct
We play at the beach yesterday.	We played at the beach yesterday.
We will jump in the waves yesterday.	We jumped in the waves yesterday.

Connect Grammar to Writing

When you revise your instructions, be sure all your verbs tell about the same time.

Reading-Writing Workshop: Revise

Write to Inform

☑ **Word Choice** It is easier for readers to follow **instructions** if the steps are clear. Choose words that tell your readers exactly what to do.

Later, Alexa revised her instructions and added exact words.

Writing Process Checklist

Prewrite

Draft

▶ **Revise**

☑ Are my steps in order?

☑ Did I use time-order words, such as *first*, *next*, and *finally*?

☑ Did I use exact words to make my steps clearer?

☑ Do I tell my readers what to do with what they made?

Edit

Publish and Share

Revised Draft

You will need a pinecone, peanut butter, birdseed, a
spoon
~~utensil~~, a paper plate, and string.

First, tie one end of the
the top
string to ~~part~~ of the pinecone.
Cut a long piece of string.

How to Make a Birdfeeder

by Alexa Saperstein

Make an easy and fun birdfeeder. You will need a pinecone, peanut butter, birdseed, a spoon, a paper plate, and string.

First, cut a long piece of string. Tie one end of the string to the top of the pinecone. Next, take a spoon, scoop some peanut butter, and spread it all over the pinecone. Then pour some birdseed on a paper plate. Roll the pinecone around in the birdseed.

I added exact words to make my instructions clearer.

Reading as a Writer

Which exact words did Alexa add to make her steps clear? Where can you add exact words to your own instructions?

Read the selection. Then read each question. Choose the best answer for the question.

Tornado!

1   Last summer, we had a scary surprise. It was a hot, humid night. It looked as if there would be a thunderstorm. Suddenly, the sky turned yellow. Then we heard a strange sound. It sounded like a train.

2   "A tornado is coming!" my dad said. My whole family ran down to the basement. We were happy when it was over. As we climbed the stairs, we began to feel <u>anxious</u>. We were about to find out what had happened.

3   A lot of trees were down. There were branches everywhere. Our neighbors had lost a part of their roof. Luckily, no one was hurt.

GO ON

1 What caused the train sound that the family heard?

  ⬭ A tornado

  ⬭ A thunderstorm

  ⬭ The yellow sky

2 How did the family probably feel when they heard the strange sound?

  ⬭ Afraid

  ⬭ Bored

  ⬭ Happy

3 What does the word <u>anxious</u> mean in paragraph 2?

  ⬭ Tired

  ⬭ Worried

  ⬭ Pleased

GO ON

Snow Day

1   It was Friday morning. Katie was still asleep. Suddenly she felt her sister jump onto her bed. Katie groaned as she looked at the clock. It was too early.

2   "Get up!" said Maddie. "You have to see this."

3   Katie got up and went to the window. She saw a strange sight. There was a lot of snow! The girls had seen a few flakes before, but this was <u>unusual</u>.

4   "Let's make a snowman!" Katie shouted.

1 Katie groans at the beginning of the story because—

    ◯   she thinks it is too early to get up

    ◯   she doesn't care about seeing the snow

    ◯   her sister has gotten her up on a weekend

2 Which word best tells how the girls feel when they see the snow?

    ◯   Unhappy

    ◯   Excited

    ◯   Lazy

3 Which word from paragraph 3 means almost the same thing as the word <u>unusual</u>?

    ◯   *strange*

    ◯   *window*

    ◯   *before*

STOP

Tell Me About It

Unit 3

Big Idea

We learn from each other.

Paired Selections

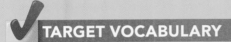

understand

gathered

impatient

impossible

believe

problem

demand

furious

Vocabulary
Reader

Context
Cards

 TEKS **2.5B** use context to determine meaning; **ELPS** **1E** internalize new basic/academic language

322

Vocabulary in Context

● Read each **Context Card**.

● Use a **Vocabulary** word to tell about something you did.

1

understand

These children talk to each other with their hands. They understand sign language.

2

gathered

The students gathered around the computer in order to see the screen.

3 impatient

This girl looks impatient. She is tired of waiting so long.

4 impossible

It is impossible to hear when there is so much noise.

5 believe

People clap if they believe, or feel, someone has done a good job.

6 problem

Raise your hand if you have a problem or need help.

7 demand

These lights and sirens demand that everyone get out of the way.

8 furious

Babies cry when they are angry. This baby is furious!

323

Background

✓ **TARGET VOCABULARY**   **Reaching an Agreement**

Students **believe** they should get a longer recess. It seems like an **impossible** wish. They should not get **impatient** or **furious**, though. They should not **demand** a longer recess, either. Once students have **gathered** with teachers, calm thinking and talking can lead to ideas. Then everyone can **understand** why a longer recess is a good plan. **Problem** solved!

How to Reach an Agreement

Present the request.

↓

Meet to discuss ideas.

↓

Agree on a solution.

TEKS 2.3A use ideas to make/confirm predictions; 2.3B ask questions/clarify/locate facts/details/support with evidence; RC-2(D) make inferences/ use textual evidence; ELPS 4J employ inferential skills to demonstrate comprehension

Comprehension

✔ TARGET SKILL Conclusions

In *Click, Clack, Moo*, the author wants you to draw conclusions. She wants you to use story clues to fill in more details than she gives. Use a chart like this to write a conclusion about Farmer Brown or his animals. List the story clues that helped.

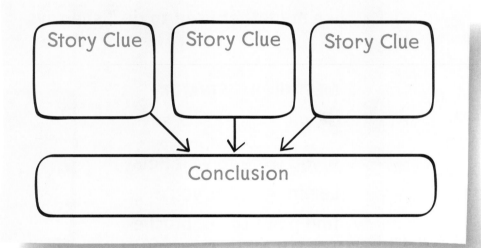

Story Clue   Story Clue   Story Clue

Conclusion

✔ TARGET STRATEGY Infer/Predict

Use your conclusions about Farmer Brown and the other animals to infer, or figure out, more about their thoughts and feelings. Your conclusions may also help you to predict what might happen next!

CLICK, CLACK, MOO
Cows That Type
by Doreen Cronin, pictures by Betsy Lewin

✔ TARGET VOCABULARY

understand	believe
gathered	problem
impatient	demand
impossible	furious

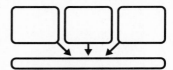
✔ TARGET SKILL

Conclusions Use details to figure out more about the text.

MEET THE AUTHOR
Doreen Cronin

When Doreen Cronin was a kid, her dad used to tell funny stories. One night several years ago, she woke up and wrote *Click, Clack, Moo*. "It made me laugh, just like my father used to do," she says.

✔ TARGET STRATEGY

Infer/Predict Use clues to figure out more about story parts.

GENRE

Humorous fiction is a story that is written to make the reader laugh.

MEET THE ILLUSTRATOR
Betsy Lewin

If you were to visit Betsy Lewin at home, you'd find paint tubes, brushes, paper, and a kitty named Sophie on her drawing table. In her travels, Ms. Lewin has seen gorillas in Uganda, elephants in Botswana, and tigers in India.

CLICK, CLACK, MOO
Cows That Type

by Doreen Cronin   **pictures by Betsy Lewin**

Essential Question

What helps you make a decision about a character?

Farmer Brown has a **problem**.

His cows like to type.

All day long he hears

Click, clack, **moo.**
  Click, clack, **moo.**
Clickety, clack, **moo.**

At first, he couldn't believe his ears.
Cows that type?
Impossible!

Click, clack, **moo.**
  Click, clack, **moo.**
Clickety, clack, **moo.**

Dear Farmer Brown,
The barn is very cold at night.
We'd like some electric blankets.
Sincerely,
The Cows

It was bad enough the cows had found the old typewriter in the barn, now they wanted electric blankets! "No way," said Farmer Brown. "No electric blankets."

So the cows went on strike. They left a note on the barn door.

Sorry.
We're closed.
No milk today.

STOP AND THINK
Conclusions How does Farmer Brown feel about the notes? How do you know?
TEKS 2.3B, RC-2(D), RC-2(F)

"No milk today!" cried Farmer Brown.
In the background, he heard the cows
busy at work:

Click, clack, **moo.**
　Click, clack, **moo.**
Clickety, clack, **moo.**

The next day, he got another note:

Dear Farmer Brown,
The hens are cold too.
They'd like electric blankets.
Sincerely,
The Cows

The cows were growing **impatient** with the farmer. They left a new note on the barn door.

"No eggs!" cried Farmer Brown. In the background he heard them.

Click, clack, **moo.**
Click, clack, **moo.**
Clickety, clack, **moo.**

"Cows that type. Hens on strike! Whoever heard of such a thing? How can I run a farm with no milk and no eggs!" Farmer Brown was **furious.**

STOP AND THINK
Author's Craft "Moo, moo" sounds like the noise a cow makes. What other sound words does the author use?

Farmer Brown got out his own typewriter.

Dear Cows and Hens:
There will be no electric blankets.
You are cows and hens.
I demand milk and eggs.
Sincerely,
Farmer Brown

Duck was a neutral party, so he brought the ultimatum to the cows.

The cows held an emergency meeting.
All the animals gathered around the
barn to snoop, but none of them could
understand Moo.

All night long, Farmer Brown waited
for an answer.

Duck knocked on the door early
the next morning. He handed
Farmer Brown a note:

Dear Farmer Brown,
We will exchange our typewriter
for electric blankets.
Leave them outside the barn door
and we will send Duck over with
the typewriter.
Sincerely,
The Cows

Farmer Brown decided this was a good deal. He left the blankets next to the barn door and waited for Duck to come with the typewriter.

342

The next morning, he got a note:

Dear Farmer Brown,
The pond is quite boring.
We'd like a diving board.
Sincerely,
The Ducks

Click, clack, **quack.**
Click, clack, **quack.**
Clickety, clack, **quack.**

STOP AND THINK

Infer/Predict Will the ducks get a diving board?
Check your prediction on the next page.

TEKS 2.3A, RC-2(D)

343

1. On page 337, the word <u>furious</u> means —

    ⊂⊃ happy

    ⊂⊃ hungry

    ⊂⊃ mad

2. ✔ **TARGET SKILL** **Conclusions**

    Why do you think Farmer Brown sends a letter to answer the cows and hens? Use a chart like this to help you answer. **TEKS** 2.9B, **ELPS** 4J

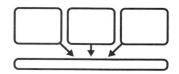

3. ✔ **TARGET STRATEGY** **Infer/Predict**

    What might happen next if the ducks gave the typewriter to some pigs? Share ideas with a partner.

    TEKS 2.3A, **ELPS** 4G

4. **Oral Language** Use the Retelling Cards to tell what happens each time Farmer Brown finds a note. **TEKS** RC-2(E), **ELPS** 3E

Retelling Cards

TEKS 2.3A use ideas to make/confirm predictions; **2.9B** describe characters' traits/motivations/feelings; **RC-2(E)** retell important story events; **ELPS** **3E** share information in cooperative learning interactions; **4G** demonstrate comprehension through shared reading/retelling/responding/note-taking; **4J** employ inferential skills to demonstrate comprehension

Talk About Smart Animals!

by Donald Logan

You may think only animals in storybooks or movies do things that seem impossible. You would be wrong!

Meet Rio and Alex. They are real-life animals. Rio is a sea lion. Alex is a parrot. These animals can do things that most people would never believe animals like them could do.

This Sea Lion Can Match

Rio is not like any other sea lion. She can solve a simple problem and tell the answer to her trainers!

Rio has learned to look at three pictures and decide which two are most alike. First, Rio's trainers show her one picture. Rio studies it. Then her trainers add two more pictures. Rio points her nose at the picture that goes best with the first one she saw. When Rio is right, she gets a tasty treat.

Rio is not impatient. She takes her time before she answers.

Rio is deciding which two of these pictures are most alike.

Not Bad for a Bird Brain!

Alex is an African grey parrot. Grey parrots in the wild are often seen gathered together in large groups. In the wild, parrots communicate using bird calls and other sounds. Alex is special because he has learned to talk. He knows over one hundred words!

Alex's owner has also taught Alex to tell colors apart and to count. Alex can even understand questions and answer them.

Sometimes Alex gets tired. He becomes furious and will demand a treat. After a break, he goes right back to solving problems.

"Want a nut!"

Making Connections

Connect to Science What can the animals in the selections do that most animals cannot do? What would you like to teach an animal to do? Explain the steps to a partner. Have your partner repeat the steps.

Compare Stories Doreen Cronin wrote *Click, Clack, Moo: Cows That Type* and *Diary of a Spider* (Lesson 4). Explain how the settings and the events of these stories are the same and different.

Write a Letter Think about the letters that the cows wrote. Write your own letter asking an adult family member for something. Be sure to include all the parts of a letter.

TEKS **2.28B** follow/restate/give oral instructions involving sequence; **2.9A** compare several works by the same author; **2.19B** write short letters using sequence/conventions; **2.20** write persuasive statements; **ELPS** **3E** share information in cooperative learning interactions; **3G** express opinions/ideas/feelings

349

Grammar

Kinds of Sentences A **statement** tells something and ends with a period. A **question** asks something and ends with a question mark. A **command** tells a person or animal to do something and ends with a period.

Academic Language

statement

question

command

Statement	Question	Command
I wrote a note.	Did you write a note?	Please write a note.

Turn and Talk **Work with a partner. Read each sentence aloud. Tell whether it is a statement, question, or command.**

❶ Have you been to a farm?

❷ She loves cows.

❸ Please share the milk.

❹ The hens lay eggs.

Sentence Fluency A run-on sentence is really two sentences that should not be joined together. If you see a run-on sentence in your writing, turn it into two shorter sentences.

Run-on Sentences	Separate Sentences
Cows are important they give us milk	Cows are important. They give us milk.
Do you drink lots of milk	Do you drink lots of milk?
I drink three glasses a day.	I drink three glasses a day.

Connect Grammar to Writing

When you revise your persuasive letter, fix run-on sentences by turning each one into two sentences.

Write to Persuade

✅ **Ideas** When you write a letter to persuade, be sure your goal is clear to your reader.

Kurt drafted a **persuasive letter**. Later, he revised it to say clearly his reason for writing. Use the Writing Traits Checklist to revise your writing.

Writing Traits Checklist

✅ **Ideas**
Did I state my goal clearly?

✅ **Organization**
Did I use the parts of a letter? Did I tell things in an order that makes sense?

✅ **Voice**
Does my writing tell how I feel?

✅ **Conventions**
Did I capitalize and punctuate the heading, greeting, and closing correctly?

Revised Draft

Dear Auntie Lorrie,

I'm writing to ask you ~~for~~ to send me some of your old children's books. ~~something.~~ It's for a really good cause.

352

3 **hours**

Learning to play an instrument well takes many hours of practice.

4 **alone**

Playing alone, or by yourself, is very special.

5 **real**

A real guitar is louder than a pretend guitar.

6 **museum**

This very old instrument is in a museum. Many people come to see it.

7 **nursery**

A nursery, or baby's room, is a good place to play soft music.

8 **whenever**

The band plays whenever the conductor signals them to.

Background

✓ TARGET VOCABULARY   **What Is a Band?** Sometimes people play music alone. Whenever people play music in a group, they form a band. Some bands play soft, smooth music. This music is good for quiet places, such as a museum or a baby's nursery. Other bands play loud, lively music. This music makes people want to shake their hands and feet and dance to the beat. Being part of a real band takes many hours of practice, but it is also lots of fun!

TEKS 2.3B ask questions/clarify/locate facts/details/support with evidence; 2.3C establish purpose/monitor comprehension; RC-2(B) ask literal questions of text; RC-2(C) monitor/adjust comprehension; ELPS 4G demonstrate comprehension through shared reading/retelling/responding/note-taking

Comprehension

✔ TARGET SKILL Story Structure

In *Violet's Music*, the main character has a problem, and she tries to solve it. Use a story map such as this one to keep track of the story structure as you read. Tell who is in the story, where it takes place, and what happens.

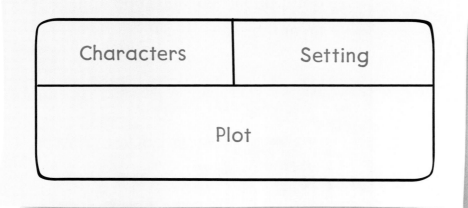

✔ TARGET STRATEGY Question

What problem does the main character face? How does she solve it? As you read, think of more questions about *Violet's Music*. Then read on to find answers. Asking and answering questions helps you make sense of the story.

shake	real
smooth	museum
hours	nursery
alone	whenever

✔ TARGET SKILL

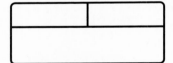

Story Structure Tell the setting, character, and plot in a story.

✔ TARGET STRATEGY

Question Ask questions about what you are reading.

GENRE
Realistic fiction is a story that could happen in real life.

MEET THE AUTHOR

Angela Johnson

As a college student, Angela Johnson used to baby-sit for Cynthia Rylant's son. One day Angela showed the famous author a story she had written. Cynthia liked it so much that she helped get it published, and soon Angela became an author, too.

MEET THE ILLUSTRATOR

Laura Huliska-Beith

Laura Huliska-Beith has held many jobs. She has been a paper carrier, a library aide, and a waitress. She almost became a bus driver. By far her favorite job is illustrating books.

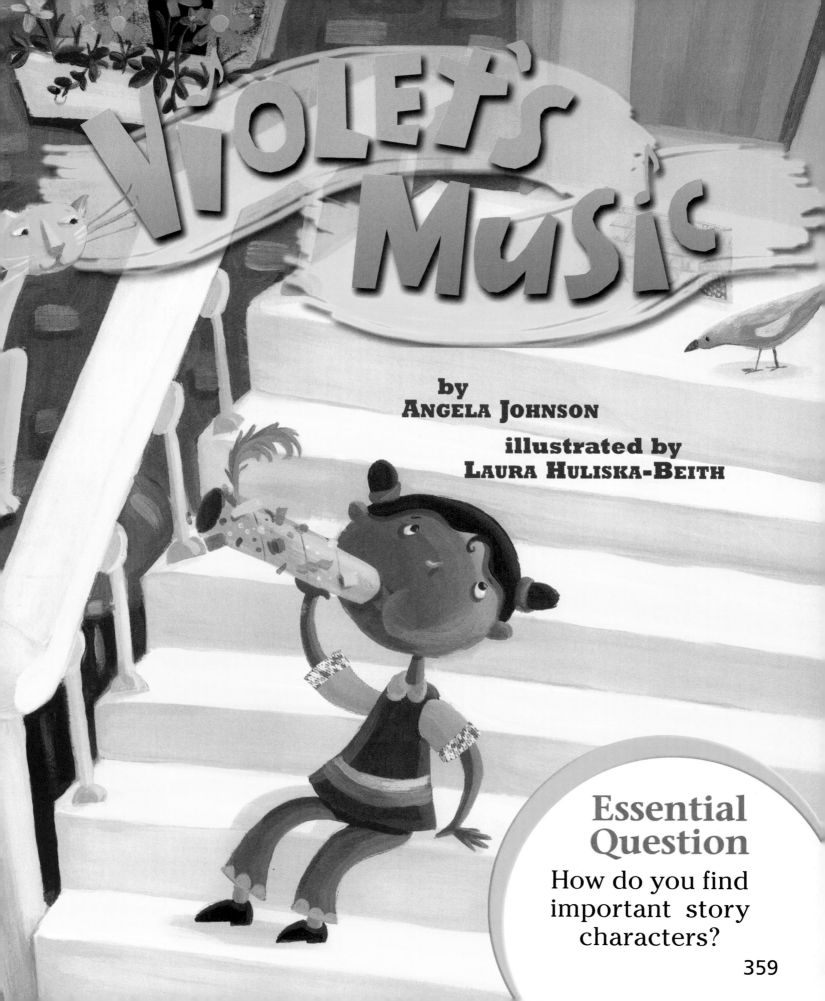

Violet's Music

by
Angela Johnson

illustrated by
Laura Huliska-Beith

Essential Question

How do you find important story characters?

When Violet was a baby, just a few hours old,
she banged her rattle against the crib,
hoping others in the nursery would join in.
    Boom
        Shake
    Beat
        Shake
All day long,
Violet played that rattle.

Could she find other babies to play along?
No, she couldn't.
But she'd keep looking.
Violet played her music all alone.

On Violet's second birthday
Aunt Bertha brought gifts
and a box full of paper, crayons,
glitter, and glue
to make horns that would wail . . .

Violet tooted from morning
till that night.

*W*HAH

Woo

Woo

All day long.

STOP AND THINK
Author's Craft Why do you think the author includes so many words that begin with *b* in the first sentence?

She tried to get everyone to toot
with her all day.

WHAH

WOO

WOO

Oh yeah.
Violet blew that horn.

Could she get her family
to play with her?
No, she couldn't.
But she'd keep on looking.
Violet blew her horn all alone.

Violet wondered in kindergarten
if there were other kids like her,
who dreamed music,
thought music,
all day long.

But she found that
some liked to paint,
some liked to paste,
others liked to play in the sandbox,
and still others just liked to stand around eating paste.

No one wanted to play music all day long.

One day at the beach
Violet played with a badminton racket,
a pretend guitar,
hoping someone would join in.

Plink

   Plink

Pluck

   Pluck

Violet played guitar.

Could she find a fellow guitarist
buried in the sand?
No, she couldn't.
But she'd keep looking.
Violet played her guitar all alone.

 **STOP AND THINK**
Question Why is it important
that Violet look for kids like her?
TEKS 2.3B

365

With Violet, you see, it was music all the time.

Breakfast time . . .

Dinner time . . .

Bath time . . .

And all times in between.

Whenever she walked down the street
or hid behind the market's vegetable bins,
or sat on the fire escape,
Violet was always looking for kids like her.

Could she find them at the zoo?
Nope.

At the 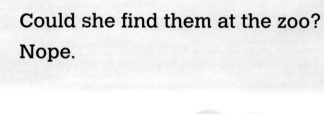museum?
Too quiet.

And forget about the dentist.

But she'd keep looking.
Violet and her music, always looking.

Until . . .
one day a few summers later,
Violet was playing her guitar
(a real one now)
in the park.

> Twang
>   Twang
> Yeah
>   Yeah
> Twang Twang
>   Yeah!

When, over by the fountain,
someone started beating a drum . . .

Then, behind the jungle gym,
a saxophone blew real smooth . . .

And over beside the flower garden,
someone started to sing . . .

 STOP AND THINK
Story Structure Where does Violet finally find kids like her?

370

Now Angel, Randy, and Juan
are in Violet's band.
And if you ask any of them
whether they thought they'd find each other,
they'll say,
"Oh, yeah, we did, we knew we would.

'Cause when we were
in the nursery,
then were two,

and later in kindergarten
and at the beach,
we kept on looking
for kids playing music too!"

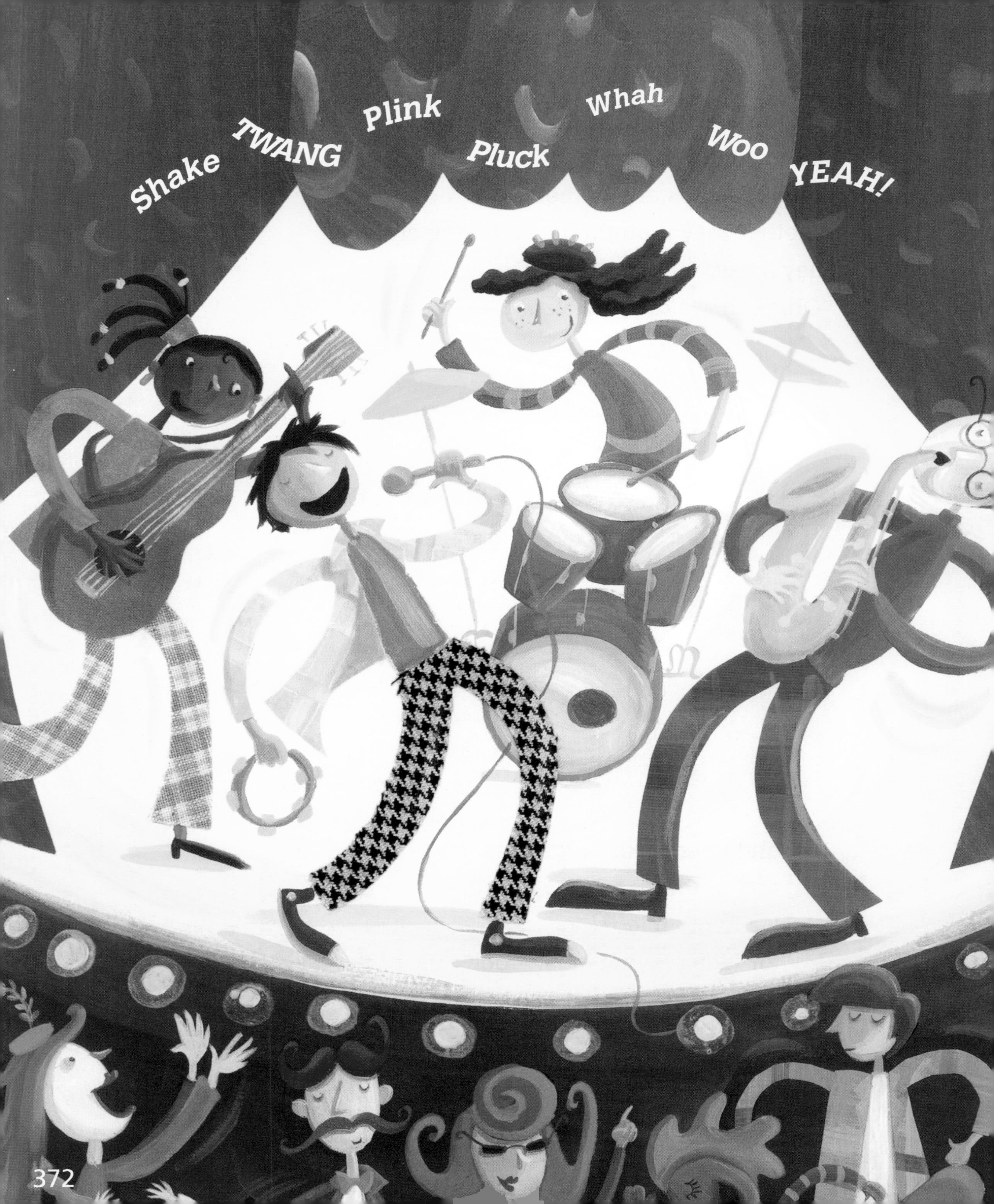
Shake
TWANG
Plink
Pluck
Whah
Woo
YEAH!

Your Turn

1. On page 360, the word <u>nursery</u> means a —

⬭ music store

⬭ baby's room

⬭ classroom

2. 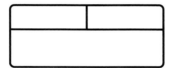 **Story Structure**

Read pages 360-365 again. Use a story map to tell about the problem Violet has.

3. **TARGET STRATEGY** **Question**

Use your story map to write a question you had about Violet. Was it answered? How?

4. Oral Language With a small group, use the Retelling Cards to act out the selection.

Retelling Cards

 TEKS 2.3B ask questions/clarify/locate facts/details/support with evidence; **ELPS 3C** speak using a variety of grammatical structures; **4I** employ reading skills to demonstrate comprehension

Wolfgang Mozart

Child Superstar
by Mark Bechelli

Most little children don't play real music.
Babies might shake a rattle in the nursery.
A five-year-old might bang a drum.

1750

1756 Wolfgang is born in this house in Austria. The house is now a museum.

Wolfgang Amadeus Mozart lived over two hundred years ago. From the time he was very young, Wolfgang was different from most children.

When Wolfgang was three, he would sit alone and play the harpsichord for hours. A harpsichord is an instrument like a piano. By the time Wolfgang was five, he could play slow and smooth or loud and fast. He even wrote his own songs all by himself!

Wolfgang Mozart's Early Life

1760

1770

1759 Wolfgang learns to play the harpsichord.

1763–1766 Wolfgang plays music all over Europe with his family.

Soon, everyone in Austria was talking about the talented child. Wolfgang played in castles and big concert halls. Whenever he performed, people were amazed. Wolfgang was becoming a musical superstar!

Wolfgang Mozart at age 6

Making Connections

 Text to Self TEKS 2.19A, ELPS 3H

Narrate a Story What does Violet like to do with her friends? Do you enjoy any of those activities with your friends? Tell a partner a story about a time you did one of these activities. Give specific details.

 Text to Text TEKS RC-2(F)

Have a Conversation Imagine you and a partner are Violet and Mozart. Have a conversation about how you are alike and different.

 Text to World TEKS RC-2(F), ELPS 3H

Connect to Social Studies Do you think that Violet likes to play music for special events? What songs do you know that people sing at special times? Discuss your ideas with a partner.

 TEKS **2.19A** write brief compositions; **RC-2(F)** make connections to experiences/texts/community; **ELPS 3H** narrate/describe/explain with detail

Grammar

Kinds of Sentences All sentences begin with capital letters. Statements and commands end with periods. Questions end with question marks. An **exclamation** shows strong feeling and ends with an **exclamation point**.

Academic Language

exclamation
exclamation point

Statement	Question	Command	Exclamation
She plays drums.	Does she play drums?	Stop playing the drums.	I love to play drums!

Try This!   **Write each sentence correctly.**

1 we are so excited to hear the band

2 what is the name of their band

3 that flute is old

4 please play a little louder

Sentence Fluency In your writing, you may use too many short, choppy sentences. You can fix this by joining sentences that go together to make one longer sentence. Write the word **and** between the sentences. Put a comma before **and**.

Short, Choppy Sentences

Lupe plays the tuba.

Her brother Jaime plays the flute.

Longer, Smoother Sentence

Lupe plays the tuba, and her brother Jaime plays the flute.

Connect Grammar to Writing

When you revise your opinion paragraph, look for short sentences that you can join with a comma and the word and.

Write to Persuade

☑ **Voice** When you write to persuade, you share your opinions with readers.

Han wrote an **opinion paragraph** about why he likes soccer. Later, he revised his draft to show how much he cares about the sport.

Writing Traits Checklist

☑ **Ideas**
Did I use details and examples to explain my reasons?

☑ **Organization**
Did I state my opinion at the beginning of my paragraph?

☑ **Voice**
Does my writing show how I feel about my subject?

☑ **Sentence Fluency**
Did I vary the length of my sentences?

Revised Draft

love
I ~~like~~ soccer. This game has something for everyone! It is easy to learn, so anyone can play. It is great exercise. People all over the world play soccer. I watch games with my brother.
each weekend

Soccer for Everyone
by Han Choi

I love soccer. This game has something for everyone! It is easy to learn, so anyone can play. It is great exercise. People all over the world play soccer. I watch games with my brother each weekend. We have so much fun when our favorite team wins. I think all children should play soccer.

I added sentences to show how I feel about my subject.

Reading as a Writer

What did Han add to let you know how he feels about his subject? What can you add to your writing to let your reader know how you feel?

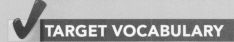

TARGET VOCABULARY

culture

community

languages

transportation

subjects

lessons

special

wear

Vocabulary
Reader

Context
Cards

Vocabulary in Context

- Read each **Context Card**.

- Talk about a picture. Use a different Vocabulary word from the one in the card.

1 culture

Culture is the traditions and beliefs of a group of people.

2 community

A community is a group of people who live together in a certain area.

3 languages

People use different languages to write and to speak to one another.

4 transportation

People use transportation to get from one place to another.

5 subjects

Science is one of the subjects taught in school.

6 lessons

This teacher gives lessons to his students. The students learn from each lesson.

7 special

These students go to a special school for music. They play music every day.

8 wear

These two students wear uniforms at school.

Background

✓ TARGET VOCABULARY   **School Days** Not all schools are the same. Some have their students wear uniforms. Some have special transportation, such as school buses. Others allow students to get their lessons over the Internet. Most schools teach different subjects. Students taking social studies may learn about their own community or a different culture. Many schools teach different languages as subjects. All schools are places where students learn!

Many American schools have classrooms like this one.

Comprehension

✔ **TARGET SKILL** **Author's Purpose**

An author may write to make you smile, to tell you facts, or to explain ideas. What is the author's purpose for writing *Schools Around the World*? Keep track of details on a chart like this one to figure out the author's purpose.

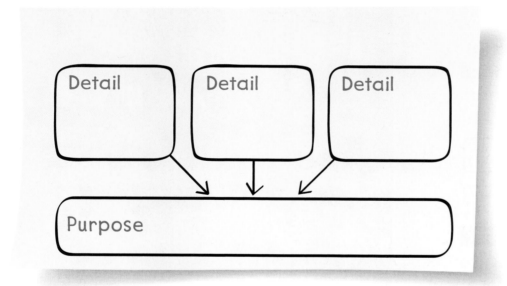

✔ **TARGET STRATEGY** **Analyze/Evaluate**

Think carefully about the selection details and the author's purpose for writing *Schools Around the World*. Use your own ideas to decide whether the author has done a good job of telling about different schools.

JOURNEYS DIGITAL Powered by DESTINATIONReading® Comprehension Activities: Lesson 13

Main Selection

TARGET VOCABULARY

culture	subjects
community	lessons
languages	special
transportation	wear

TARGET SKILL

Author's Purpose
Tell why an author writes a book.

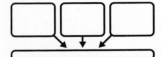

TARGET STRATEGY

Analyze/Evaluate
Tell how you feel about the text, and why.

GENRE
Informational Text
gives facts about a topic. Set a purpose for reading based on the genre.

 TEKS 2.3C establish purpose/monitor comprehension

MEET THE AUTHOR

Margaret C. Hall

Margaret C. Hall has written many nonfiction books for children. Her books include topics from national parks to mallard ducks. *Schools Around the World* is part of a series of books she wrote. Other books in the series include *Homes Around the World* and *Games Around the World*.

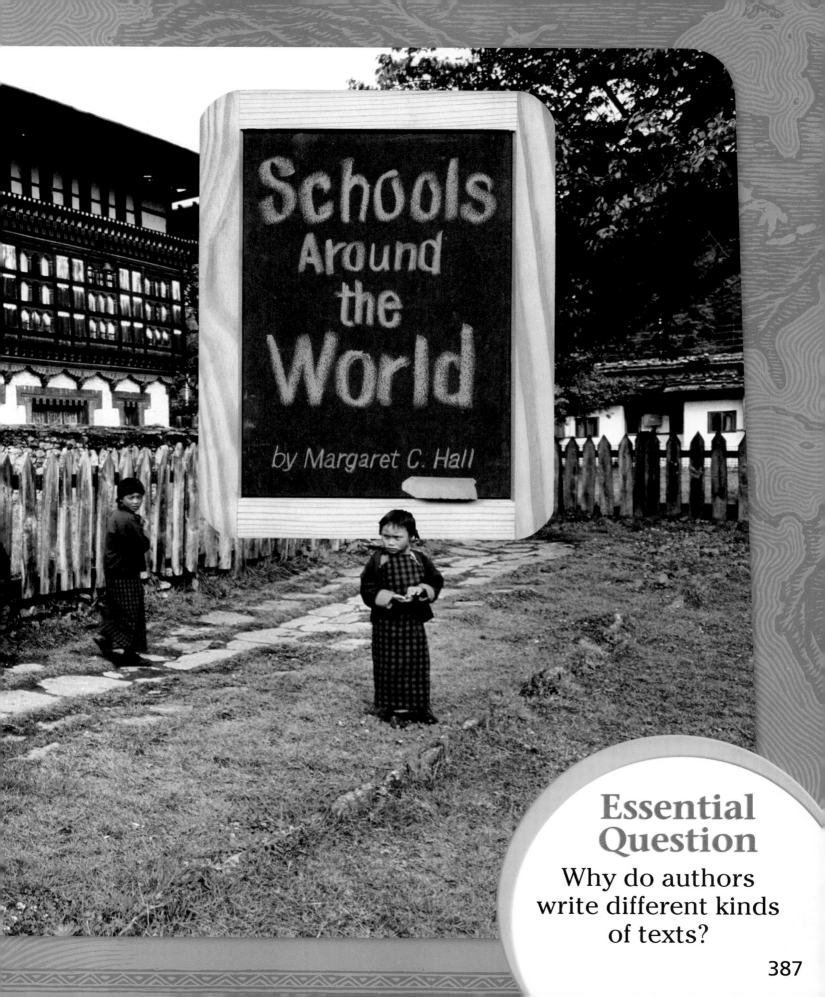

Schools Around the World

by Margaret C. Hall

Essential Question

Why do authors write different kinds of texts?

Schools Around the World

All around the world, children go to school.
Some children spend most of their day at school.
Others spend only a few hours there.

Some school buildings in Asia are tall, like this one.

These students in an American classroom start their day by saying the Pledge of Allegiance.

Schools are different in different parts of the world. But they are all the same in one way. Schools are where children go to learn.

AMAZING SCHOOL FACTS

A long time ago, a German man started a new kind of school. He thought that small children should grow like flowers in a garden. He called his school kindergarten. The word means "children's garden" in German.

These students in Tibet, China, are about to start their morning classes.

School Buildings

The kind of school buildings children have depends on where they live. It depends on the climate and the resources of their community.

School buildings can be large or small. They can be made from many different materials. Some children even go to school outside or in buildings with no walls.

AMAZING SCHOOL FACTS

Schools have been around for thousands of years. The first schools were started to teach children about their culture.

Getting to School

Children travel to school in many different ways. The kind of transportation they use depends on where they live. It also depends on how far they have to go.

Many children walk or ride bicycles to school. Others ride in cars, on buses, or on a train. Some children go to school by boat.

AMAZING SCHOOL FACTS

In some places, children live too far away from their school to go there. Teachers give lessons over the radio or by using computers that are hooked up to the school.

✔ **STOP AND THINK**

Author's Purpose Do you think the author is trying to tell facts or tell a story about transportation? Explain.

TEKS 2.13

This teacher answers a question for his student at a school in Cuba.

Learning to Read and Write

One important job for teachers is to help children learn to read and write. Students learn to read and write in many different languages. The language children use at school depends on where they live. Some children study their own language and another language, too.

STOP AND THINK
Author's Craft How do the captions help the author tell about different schools?

At an American school overseas, students study a map of Europe.

Other Lessons

Children learn many things at school. All around the world, they study math and science. They learn about their own country and other countries, too.

Many children around the world study art and music in school. They may also learn how to use a computer.

These students in Great Britain practice playing music at school.

In this school in Japan, students help serve lunch.

School Chores

Most children have chores to do at school. They help to keep the classroom neat and clean. They may even help to set up the classroom every day.

In some places, children work to keep the schoolyard neat and clean. Some children may serve lunch to one another.

This teacher gives extra help to students after school.

After School

Some children go to school even after the school day is over. They may have a tutor to help them with the subjects that are harder for them.

Some children have other lessons after school. They study things they cannot learn in school. They may learn about dance, music, or their own culture.

These boys in Israel learn about their culture.

Students at this boarding school eat, study, and live together.

Special Schools

Some children live at their schools. These schools are called boarding schools. The children go home for visits and on holidays.

This girl cannot see. She goes to a school where she can learn to read and write in a special way. People who are blind read with their fingers. They use a system of raised dots called Braille.

Home Schooling

A home can also be a school. Some parents teach their children at home. They want to decide exactly what their children will learn.

People at schools will often help parents plan home lessons for their children. Many children who study at home go to a school for gym or art classes.

This mother is teaching her daughter at home.

School and Work

Some children work as performers. They spend part of their day practicing the work that they do. They spend the rest of the day studying regular school subjects.

The students below perform a traditional Russian dance.

One of the subjects that was taught in ancient Greece was gymnastics. The ancient Greeks thought gymnastics was just as important to learn as math or reading!

This boy is learning gymnastics.

Older Students

These women in India go to school at night.

Many people go to school even after they are adults. They may go to college. Or, they may go to a trade school to learn how to do a certain job.

Adults also take classes for fun. They study different languages and learn how to do things. No matter how old students are, they go to school to learn.

✔ STOP AND THINK
Analyze/Evaluate Is it good for adults to go to school? Why or why not?

Your Turn

1. The section "School Chores" is mostly about —

   ⬭ jobs children have in school

   ⬭ how to clean up a classroom

   ⬭ children who serve lunch to other students

   TEKS 2.14A

2. 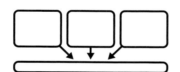 **Author's Purpose**

   Why do you think the author wrote the section "Getting to School"? Use a chart like this to list text details to answer the question. **TEKS** 2.3B, 2.13

   [chart diagram: three boxes with arrows pointing down to a single box]

3. **TARGET STRATEGY** **Analyze/Evaluate**

   Which school fact was most interesting to you? Tell why you liked it, using details from the text to support your ideas. **TEKS** 2.3B

4. **Oral Language** Work with a partner. Use the Retelling Cards to retell facts from the selection. **TEKS** 2.3B, **ELPS** 3H

Retelling Cards

 TEKS 2.3B ask questions/clarify/locate facts/details; **2.13** identify topic/explain author's purpose; **2.14A** identify main idea/distinguish from topic; **ELPS 3H** narrate/describe/explain with detail

School Poems

You learn about many subjects in school. You may have lessons in math, about your community, or even about another culture.

The poems here are about school. Listen for rhythm and rhyming words as you read.

School

Wakes up early.
Just can't wait
to see who's coming.
Don't be late!

by Dee Lillegard

The Best

The best part
of the day
is when I hear
the teacher say,
"Sit by my chair
while I read."

We sprawl
on the rug.
It's like listening
to a hug,
while the story magic
pours over me.

by Kay Winters

I Have to Write a Poem for Class

I have to write a poem for class
But don't think I'll succeed.
I know I don't know all the words
That I am going to need.
I cannot quite imagine
How my poem's supposed to be —
I've got a sinking feeling
I'm not good at poetry.

My poem must have a meter,
And it also has to rhyme.
It's due tomorrow morning . . .
How I wish I had more time!
I do not think that I can write
A poem the way I should —
But look . . . this is a poem right here,
And it is pretty good.

by Jack Prelutsky

Write a School Poem

Use rhyming words and rhythm to write your own poem about school. Try to include the words wear, transportation, languages, and special in your poem.

Making Connections

 Text to Self

Draw and Label Fold a piece of paper in half. Draw a school from *Schools Around the World* on one half. Draw your own school on the other half. Write a label on each picture that describes the school.

 Text to Text

Write a Poem Choose one of the headings from *Schools Around the World* as a topic for a poem. Then choose two rhyming words from the poems in "School Poems." Use the rhyming words to write a poem about the topic you chose.

 Text to World

Connect to Social Studies With a small group, choose one of the countries you read about in *Schools Around the World*. Use books and other sources to find out more about schools in that country. Make a poster that shows what you learn.

 TEKS 2.27 create visual display/dramatization to present research; **RC-2(F)** make connections to experiences/texts/community

Grammar

Quotation Marks When you write, show what someone says by putting **quotation marks** (" ") at the beginning and end of the speaker's exact words.

Academic Language

quotation marks

comma

capital letter

end mark

Rules for Using Quotation Marks

Put a **comma** after words such as *said* and *asked*.

The teacher said, "Take out your math books."

Begin the first word inside the quotation marks with a **capital letter**.

Mike said, "We are having a quiz today."

Put the **end mark** inside the quotation marks.

Liza asked, "Who is the class leader?"

Try This! **Write each sentence correctly. Include quotation marks to show the exact words someone said or asked.**

1. The bus driver said stay in your seats.

2. Jack asked how long is the trip?

3. The teacher said it will take an hour.

Conventions You have read stories in which people talk to each other. This makes a story more interesting. Make your own writing more interesting by showing the words people speak.

Quotation Marks

Nita asked, "What is your favorite subject in school?"
Raj said, "My favorite subject is science."

Connect Grammar to Writing

When you edit your persuasive paragraph, be sure to use commas, capital letters, and end marks correctly.

Write to Persuade

✔ **Word Choice** When you write to persuade, use exact words to make your writing more interesting.

Rachel wrote a **persuasive paragraph** asking her teacher to take her class to a museum. Later, she revised her writing to use more exact words. Use exact words when you edit your paragraph.

Writing Traits Checklist

✔ **Organization**
Did I state my opinion at the beginning?

✔ **Word Choice**
Did I use exact words to make my writing interesting?

✔ **Voice**
Did I choose reasons that are important to my audience?

✔ **Sentence Fluency**
Did I begin my sentences in different ways?

Revised Draft

Our class should go to the Children's Museum.

The Children's Museum has
~~lots of nice~~ many wonderful displays. One display shows how food gets from the farm to the market. We're learning about that in Social Studies right now.

Let's Take a Trip!

by Rachel Wollmer

Our class should go to the Children's Museum. The Children's Museum has many wonderful displays. One display shows how food gets from the farm to the market. We're learning about that in Social Studies right now. We could write a research paper about what we learn at the museum. Everyone would have a fun day together, too!

> I used exact words to make my writing interesting to my readers.

Reading as a Writer

Which exact words did Rachel add? What words can you add to make your writing more interesting?

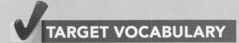

✔ **TARGET VOCABULARY**

knowledge

curious

motion

silence

illness

imitated

darkness

behavior

Vocabulary Reader | Context Cards

 TEKS 2.5B use context to determine meaning; **ELPS** 4F use visual/contextual/peer/ teacher support to read/comprehend texts

Vocabulary in Context

● Read each **Context Card**.

● Ask a partner a question that uses one of the Vocabulary words.

1 **knowledge**

Knowledge, or information, can come from books and many other places.

2 **curious**

You can search the Internet if you are curious, or want to learn, about sea animals.

3 motion

A hand held up is a **motion** to stop!

4 silence

The rule in the library is "**Silence**! Please don't speak."

5 illness

This child has an **illness**, but she won't be sick for long.

6 imitated

This girl **imitated**, or copied, her teacher to learn sign language.

7 darkness

Flashlights help people see better in **darkness**.

8 behavior

Taking a telephone message is good **behavior**. It is a polite way to act.

Background

✔ **TARGET VOCABULARY** **Braille and Keller** Louis Braille was a curious child. Risky behavior led to an accident and an illness that took away his sight. In school Louis had to read books to gain knowledge. He created a writing system he could read through the motion of his fingertips across a page. Years later, Helen Keller's life imitated Louis's in some ways. Helen lived in both darkness and silence. Reading books with the system Braille invented helped her learn about the world.

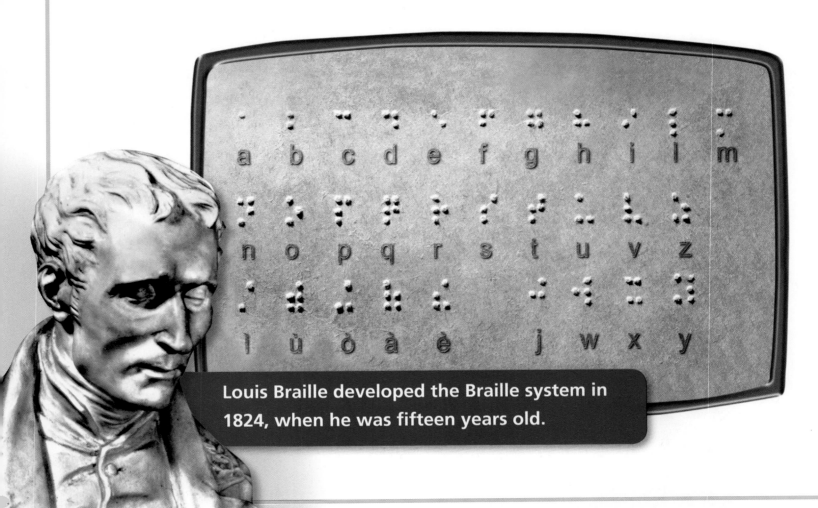

Louis Braille developed the Braille system in 1824, when he was fifteen years old.

TEKS 2.13 identify topic/explain author's purpose; **2.14A** identify main idea/distinguish from topic; **2.14B** locate facts in text; **ELPS** 4G demonstrate comprehension through shared reading/retelling/responding/note-taking

Comprehension

✔ TARGET SKILL Main Ideas and Details

When you read *Helen Keller*, you will learn details about her childhood. Use those details to figure out main, or important, ideas that the author gives. Show a main idea about Helen's life on a chart like this. List the details that make the main idea clearer.

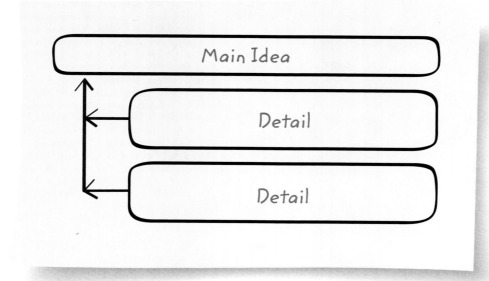

✔ TARGET STRATEGY Summarize

As you read, use the main ideas to summarize the important parts of Helen's life. Then use your summary to figure out the topic. Tell how the topic is different from the main idea.

TARGET VOCABULARY

knowledge	illness
curious	imitated
motion	darkness
silence	behavior

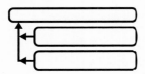

TARGET SKILL

Main Ideas and Details Tell important ideas and details about a topic.

TARGET STRATEGY

Summarize Stop to tell important ideas as you read.

GENRE

A **biography** tells about events in a person's life.

MEET THE AUTHOR

Jane Sutcliffe

The library was Jane Sutcliffe's favorite place to visit when she was a kid. She says she loved reading biographies "just to get a peek at how other people lived day to day, in different times and places." Now she writes biographies.

MEET THE ILLUSTRATOR

Robert Papp

Most of Robert Papp's clothes are covered in oil paint. That's because he's extremely messy when he paints. Mr. Papp lives in Pennsylvania with his wife, Lisa, who is also an artist. She's not quite as messy as he is, though.

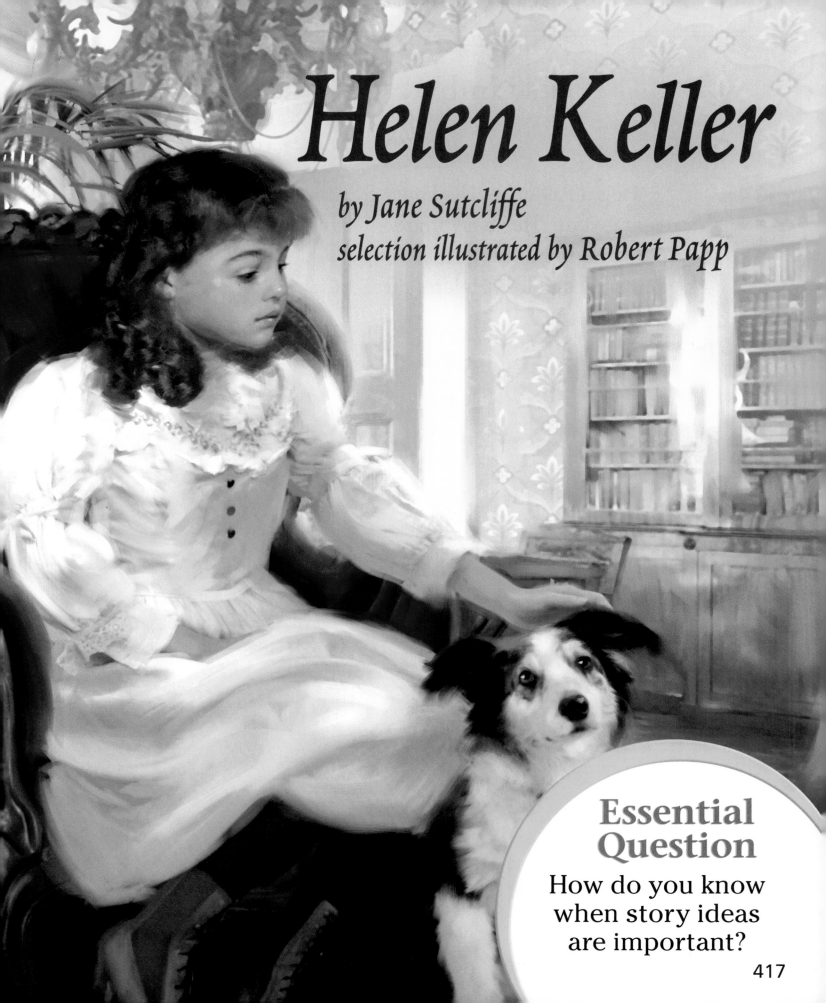

Helen Keller

by Jane Sutcliffe

selection illustrated by Robert Papp

Essential Question

How do you know when story ideas are important?

Tuscumbia, Alabama
1886

Helen Keller reached out. She touched warm, coarse hair. Her busy fingers moved farther down. They felt something smooth and wet. Slap! A hairy tail smacked into Helen's face.

Helen could not see her family's milking cow. But she liked touching it. Helen Keller had been blind and deaf for most of her life. The only way she knew the world was by touch, taste, and smell.

Helen was born in 1880 in Tuscumbia, Alabama. When she was just a baby, she became very sick. The illness took away her sight and hearing. Helen could not hear her brothers' laughter or her mother's voice. She could not see her father's smile or the pretty flowers outside her window. For Helen, there was only silence and gray darkness.

To learn to speak, children need to hear words. But Helen could not hear anything. So she could not speak. Instead, she made motions. When she wanted her mother, she put her hand against her face. When she wanted her father, she made the motion of putting on a pair of glasses. When she was hungry, she pretended to slice and butter bread.

Helen Keller

Helen knew she was different from the rest of her family. They moved their lips when they wanted things. Sometimes Helen stood between two people as they talked. She held her hands to their lips. Then she tried moving her own lips. But still no one understood her.

 STOP AND THINK

Main Ideas and Details How did Helen know that she was different from the rest of her family?

TEKS 2.14B

That made Helen angry. Sometimes she screamed and cried and kicked for hours. She threw things and hit people. But it didn't change anything. She was still alone in silence and darkness.

Helen was hard to control. Her parents didn't know how to help her. They took her to doctors. None of the doctors could help Helen see or hear again. When Helen was six, a doctor suggested the Kellers visit Alexander Graham Bell. Dr. Bell was famous for inventing the telephone. He also taught deaf people.

Alexander Graham Bell

Dr. Bell told the Kellers to write to Michael Anagnos in Boston. Mr. Anagnos was the head of the Perkins Institution for the Blind. He believed Helen could learn how to let out the thoughts locked inside her. Mr. Anagnos promised to send Helen a teacher.

Michael Anagnos

Helen and Teacher
March 1887

Helen's teacher came to live with the Kellers that spring. Her name was Annie Sullivan. Annie had studied at the Perkins School. She was nearly blind herself. Annie needed to control Helen's wild behavior so she could teach her. But Helen did not understand that Annie wanted to help her. For two weeks, Helen fought with Annie. She hit Annie and knocked out one of her front teeth. She even locked Annie in an upstairs room. Mr. Keller had to get a ladder and let Annie out through a window.

Annie Sullivan

Still, Annie did not give up. Little by little, Helen learned to trust her new teacher. Annie began to teach Helen about words. She spelled words using her fingers. Her hand formed a different shape for each letter. She pressed each shape into Helen's hand. When she gave Helen some cake, she spelled C-A-K-E into Helen's palm. When Helen held her doll, Annie spelled D-O-L-L for Helen. Helen imitated the shapes. She thought it was a game. She didn't know that the shapes spelled words.

After a month, Helen could spell whatever Annie spelled. But Helen still did not know that she was naming the things she touched.

STOP AND THINK
Summarize How did Annie teach Helen about words?

Annie finger spelling into Helen's hand

One day Helen and Annie walked to the well house. Someone was pumping water. Annie pushed Helen's hand into the rushing water. Helen felt the cool water on one hand. She felt her teacher's fingers spelling W-A-T-E-R into her other hand. Over and over, Annie spelled the word. Suddenly Helen stood very still. All at once she understood! The liquid flowing over her hand had a name. It was W-A-T-E-R!

Everything had a name! Helen wanted to learn them all. She ran from one thing to another. Annie spelled the name of everything Helen touched. Then Helen turned and pointed to Annie. T-E-A-C-H-E-R, spelled Annie. From then on, Helen's name for Annie was "Teacher." That summer, Helen learned a lot of new words. She stopped using her old motions. Her fingers gave her all the words she needed.

Annie did not teach Helen words one at a time. She talked to her in full sentences. That way, Helen learned more than just new words. She learned new ideas. Helen and Annie took long walks through the woods and along the river. Annie gave Helen lessons on the walks. She showed Helen how seeds sprout and plants grow. She made mountains out of mud and taught Helen about volcanoes. Sometimes they climbed a tree and had a lesson there.

Helen and Annie having a lesson

Reading a book in Braille

Helen was hungry for knowledge. She wanted to learn everything Annie could teach her. Soon Annie started teaching Helen how to read. The words were printed in raised letters for a blind person.

Helen felt the words with her fingers. She liked to hunt for words she knew. When she learned to read better, she read her books over and over. Her curious fingers wore down the raised letters.

STOP AND THINK
Author's Craft What does "hungry" mean in the first sentence?
TEKS 2.11

Helen also learned to write. She wrote letters to her family and Dr. Bell. She wrote many letters to Mr. Anagnos in Boston. Mr. Anagnos was amazed by how much Helen had learned. He published some of Helen's letters. Reporters began to write about Helen. Soon she was famous. People all over the world wanted to know about the miracle girl. And Helen wanted to know all about the world.

Your Turn

1. What happened after Helen's family sent a letter to Mr. Anagnos?

   ⬭ Helen went to see Alexander Graham Bell.

   ⬭ Helen got a teacher.

   ⬭ Helen became blind.

2. ✔ **TARGET SKILL** **Main Ideas and Details**

   What is the main idea on pages 428–429? What details tell more about it? Use a chart like this to show the main idea and details. **ELPS** 4I

   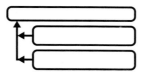

3. ✔ **TARGET STRATEGY** **Summarize**

   Summarize how Helen's life changes after she learns how words work. **TEKS** 2.14C, **ELPS** 4G

4. **Oral Language** Work with a partner. Retell how Helen changed. **TEKS** 2.14C, **ELPS** 3B

 TEKS 2.14C describe order of events/ideas in text; **ELPS** 3B expand/internalize initial English vocabulary; 4G demonstrate comprehension through shared reading/retelling/responding/note-taking; 4I employ reading skills to demonstrate comprehension

✓ TARGET VOCABULARY

knowledge	illness
curious	imitated
motion	darkness
silence	behavior

GENRE

Informational text gives facts about a topic. This is a science text.

TEXT FOCUS

Photographs show true pictures of important details. **Captions** tell more information about the photo.

Talking TOOLS

Helen Keller lived in darkness, but she was curious about the world. Braille helped Keller gain knowledge. Today people who cannot see still use Braille to help them read.

Many ATMs (Automated Teller Machines) have Braille labels, for example. That way, blind people can use them to do their banking.

Some ATMs even talk! With just one quick motion, users plug headphones into the ATM. Then the ATM tells them what to do.

A Braille notetaker is a computer that helps people who cannot see. They type their notes on it, using a Braille keyboard. The notes are saved in Braille. Later they can use their fingers to read the notes in silence on the notepad. The machine can also read the notes aloud!

This girl is using a Braille notetaker. It uses an imitated human voice to read aloud.

speaker

notepad

dot keys

What if someone who cannot see has an illness and needs to take a temperature? Use a talking thermometer! There are talking clocks and watches as well. These watches often have Braille faces, too.

If Helen Keller were alive today, she'd be happy to learn of the many ways technology can help people with vision disabilities.

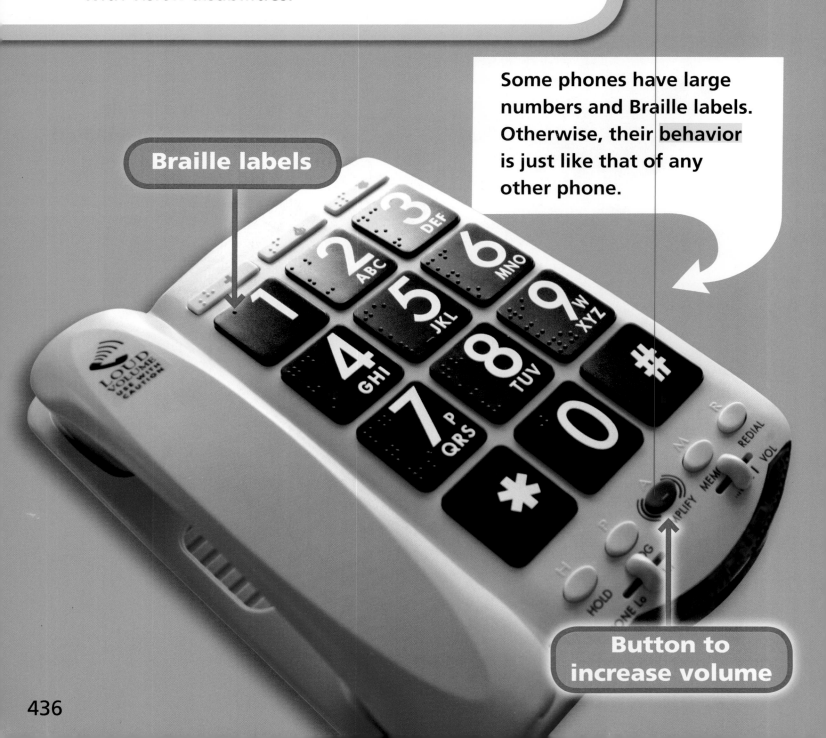

Some phones have large numbers and Braille labels. Otherwise, their behavior is just like that of any other phone.

Braille labels

Button to increase volume

Making Connections

 Text to Self
TEKS 2.30, ELPS 2G

Discuss Learning Think of some things that Annie taught Helen. Talk with a group about the way you learned these same lessons and how that is different from the way Helen learned. Take turns listening and speaking about the topic. Speak only when it is your turn.

 Text to Text

Connect to Technology Which of the tools from "Talking Tools" do you think Helen would have liked to use the most? Share your ideas with a partner.

 Text to World
TEKS 2.20

Write a Paragraph Use an encyclopedia or other information source to locate facts about the Braille equipment in "Talking Tools." Clarify that information by asking questions. Then write a paragraph about ways your town can help blind community members.

 TEKS 2.20 write persuasive statements; **2.30** follow discussion rules; **ELPS** 2G understand meaning/main points/details of spoken language

437

Grammar

Using Proper Nouns Names for **days** of the week and **months** begin with capital letters. Each important word in the name of a **holiday** begins with a capital letter, too.

Academic Language

days

months

holiday

Days	Months	Holidays
Monday	March	New Year's Day
Friday	July	Thanksgiving Day
Saturday	September	Fourth of July

Try This! **Write each sentence correctly.**

1 Is labor day in september?

2 valentine's day is in february.

3 This monday is earth day.

4 I gave my mother flowers on mother's day.

Ideas In your writing, use days, holidays, and dates to tell your reader more about when things happen. Remember to begin the names of days, months, and holidays with a capital letter.

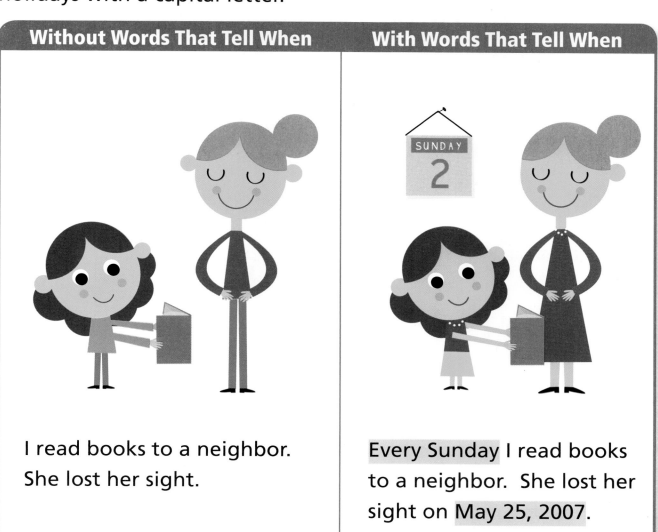

Without Words That Tell When	With Words That Tell When
I read books to a neighbor. She lost her sight.	Every Sunday I read books to a neighbor. She lost her sight on May 25, 2007.

✏ Connect Grammar to Writing

As you revise your persuasive essay next week, think about ways to tell your reader more. Add words that tell when.

Reading-Writing Workshop: Prewrite

Write to Persuade

☑ **Ideas** When you write to persuade, give your readers reasons to support your goal.

Farah made a web to plan her **persuasive essay**. She had two reasons. Later, she added details and facts to make her reasons stronger.

Writing Process Checklist

▶ **Prewrite**

☑ **Did I choose a goal I care about?**

☑ **Did I give reasons that support my goal?**

☑ **Did I include details and facts to make my reasons convincing to my audience?**

Draft

Revise

Edit

Publish and Share

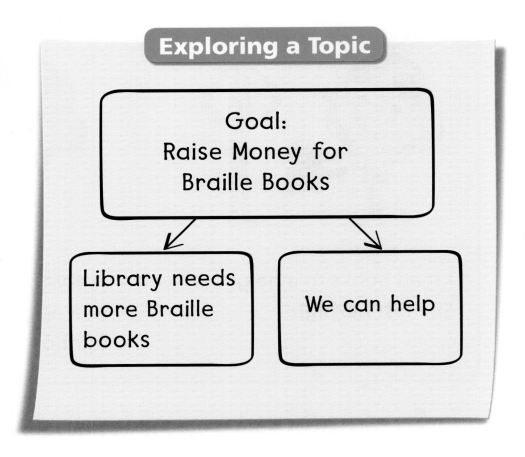

Exploring a Topic

Goal:
Raise Money for
Braille Books

Library needs more Braille books

We can help

440

Idea Web

```
          Goal: Raise Money
          for Braille Books
         ↙                    ↘
Library needs              We can help
more Braille books
  ↙          ↘            ↙          ↘
Many      Library      Our        We can
people    has only     school     do a
in town   20           wants a    Read-
read      Braille      community  a-thon
Braille   books        project
```

I added supporting details to make my reasons more convincing.

Reading as a Writer

What details did Farah add? What details can you add to make your reasons more persuasive?

441

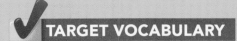

obeys

safety

attention

buddy

station

speech

shocked

enormous

Vocabulary
Reader

Context
Cards

 TEKS 2.5B use context to determine meaning; **ELPS** 1E internalize new basic/academic language

Vocabulary in Context

● Read each **Context Card**.

● Tell a story about two pictures, using the Vocabulary words.

1 **obeys**

A careful driver always obeys traffic rules. This driver stops at a stop sign.

2 **safety**

The firefighter talks about fire safety. He teaches about staying out of danger.

3 attention

Look both ways and pay attention to traffic before crossing the street.

4 buddy

Never swim alone. Always swim with a buddy, or friend.

5 station

A police station is a safe place to go if you need help.

6 speech

His job is to give a short speech. He will talk about airplane safety.

7 shocked

She is shocked at how hot it is outside. She needs to get out of the sun soon!

8 enormous

Only the workers can go inside the fence on this enormous work site.

Background

✓ **TARGET VOCABULARY** **Police Officers** Whether they work in an enormous city or a small town, police officers do an important job. They make sure everyone obeys the law. Some officers work at a police station. Others go on patrol with a buddy. Officers may visit a school to give a speech. You should pay attention to their safety tips. Officers are not shocked by questions they get asked. They have seen many things on the job!

This is a map of a police station.

Locker Room

Storage Room

Meeting Room

Interview Room

Front Desk

Waiting Area

Main Entrance

Parking lot for police vehicles

Comprehension

✔ TARGET SKILL Cause and Effect

In *Officer Buckle and Gloria*, some events make other things happen. The first event is the cause. The event that is the result of a cause is its effect. Show how the events connect to each other on a chart like this one.

Cause	Effect

✔ TARGET STRATEGY Monitor/Clarify

When you read, monitor your understanding of story events. If you don't understand why something is happening, stop and think. Looking for causes and effects can help you understand the story better.

✔ TARGET SKILL

Cause and Effect Tell how one event makes another happen.

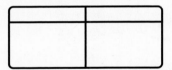

✔ TARGET STRATEGY

Monitor/Clarify Find ways to figure out what doesn't make sense.

GENRE

Humorous fiction is a story that is written to make the reader laugh.

MEET THE AUTHOR AND ILLUSTRATOR

PEGGY RATHMANN

Peggy Rathmann's family had a dog named Skippy. One holiday they were gathered for breakfast. A family member was filming them. It wasn't until later when they were watching the home movie that they caught Skippy in the background, licking the poached eggs on the serving table. No one had seen it happen. Skippy was the model for the dog in *Officer Buckle and Gloria*.

OFFICER BUCKLE

AND

GLORIA

written and illustrated by
PEGGY RATHMANN

Essential Question

What might cause a story character to change?

447

Officer Buckle knew more safety tips than anyone else in Napville.

Every time he thought of a new one, he thumbtacked it to his bulletin board.

Safety Tip #77

NEVER stand on a SWIVEL CHAIR.

Officer Buckle shared his safety tips with the students at Napville School.

Nobody ever listened.

Sometimes, there was snoring.

Afterward, it was business as usual.

Mrs. Toppel, the principal, took down the welcome banner.

"NEVER stand on a SWIVEL CHAIR," said Officer Buckle, but Mrs. Toppel didn't hear him.

Then one day, Napville's police department bought a police dog named Gloria.

When it was time for Officer Buckle to give the safety speech at the school, Gloria went along.

"Children, this is Gloria," announced Officer Buckle. "Gloria obeys my commands. Gloria, SIT!" And Gloria sat.

Officer Buckle gave Safety Tip Number One:
"KEEP your SHOELACES tied!"
The children sat up and stared.

Officer Buckle checked to see if Gloria was
sitting at attention. She was.

"Safety Tip Number Two," said Officer Buckle. "ALWAYS wipe up spills BEFORE someone SLIPS AND FALLS!"

The children's eyes popped.

Officer Buckle checked on Gloria again.

"Good dog," he said.

Officer Buckle thought of a safety tip he had discovered that morning.

"NEVER leave a THUMBTACK where you might SIT on it!"
The audience roared.

Officer Buckle grinned. He said the rest of the tips with *plenty of* expression.

The children clapped their hands and cheered. Some of them laughed until they cried.

Officer Buckle was surprised. He had never noticed how funny safety tips could be.

After *this* safety speech, there wasn't a single accident.

✔ **STOP AND THINK**
Cause and Effect What do the children do when Gloria acts out Officer Buckle's safety tips?

TEKS 2.3B

455

The next day, an enormous envelope arrived
at the police station. It was stuffed with thank-you
letters from the students at Napville School.

Every letter had a drawing of Gloria on it.

Officer Buckle thought the drawings showed a
lot of imagination.

 **STOP AND THINK**

Monitor/Clarify Why does Officer
Buckle think the students' drawings
show a lot of imagination?

TEKS RC-2(C)

His favorite letter was written on a star-shaped piece of paper. It said:

You and Gloria make a good team.

Your friend,
Claire

P.S. I always wear a crash helmet.
(Safety Tip #7)

Officer Buckle was thumbtacking Claire's letter to his bulletin board when the phones started ringing. Grade schools, high schools, and day-care centers were calling about the safety speech.

"Officer Buckle," they said, "our students want to hear your safety tips! And please, bring along that police dog."

Officer Buckle told his safety tips to 313 schools.
Everywhere he and Gloria went, children sat up
and listened.

After every speech, Officer Buckle took Gloria out for ice cream.

Officer Buckle loved having a buddy.

459

Then one day, a television news team videotaped
Officer Buckle in the state-college auditorium.

When he finished Safety Tip Number Ninety-nine,
DO NOT GO SWIMMING DURING ELECTRICAL
STORMS!, the students jumped to their feet and
applauded.

"Bravo! Bravo!" they cheered. Officer
Buckle bowed again and again.

STOP AND THINK
Author's Craft The author uses
capital letters for some words. Why?

That night, Officer Buckle watched himself
on the 10 o'clock news.

The next day, the principal of Napville School
telephoned the police station.

"Good morning, Officer Buckle! It's time for
our safety speech!"

Officer Buckle frowned.

"I'm not giving any more speeches! Nobody
looks at me, anyway!"

"Oh," said Mrs. Toppel. "Well! How about
Gloria? Could she come?"

Someone else from the police station gave Gloria a ride to the school.

Gloria sat onstage looking lonely. Then she fell asleep. So did the audience.

After Gloria left, Napville School had its biggest accident ever . . .

It started with a puddle of banana pudding. . . .
SPLAT! SPLATTER! SPLOOSH!

Everyone slid smack into Mrs. Toppel, who screamed and let go of her hammer.

465

The next morning, a pile of letters arrived at the police station.

Every letter had a drawing of the accident.

Officer Buckle was shocked.

At the bottom of the pile was a note written on a paper star.

Officer Buckle smiled. The note said:

Gloria missed you yesterday!
Your friend,
Claire

P.S. Don't worry, I was wearing my helmet!
(Safety Tip #7)

Gloria gave Officer Buckle a big kiss on the nose.

Officer Buckle gave Gloria a nice pat on the back.

Then, Officer Buckle thought of his best safety tip yet . . .

Safety Tip #101

"ALWAYS STICK WITH YOUR BUDDY!"

YourTurn

1. How does Officer Buckle feel about having Gloria for a buddy?

   ⬭ Happy

   ⬭ Worried

   ⬭ Sleepy

   TEKS 2.9B

2. 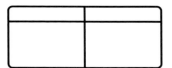 **TARGET SKILL** **Cause and Effect**

   What causes the children to listen to Officer Buckle? List the causes and effects. **TEKS** RC-2(E)

3. **TARGET STRATEGY** **Monitor/Clarify**

   How do the text and art explain why Officer Buckle does not want to give speeches anymore?
   TEKS 2.3B, 2.9B, 2.16B, **ELPS** 4K

4. **Oral Language** Use the Retelling Cards to tell the beginning, middle, and end of the story. **TEKS** RC-2(E)

   Retelling Cards

 TEKS **2.3B** ask questions/clarify/locate facts/details/support with evidence; **2.9B** describe characters' traits/motivations/feelings; **2.16B** describe media message techniques; **RC-2(E)** retell important story events; **ELPS 4K** employ analytical skills to demonstrate comprehension

Safety at Home

✔ **TARGET VOCABULARY**

obeys	station
safety	speech
attention	shocked
buddy	enormous

GENRE

Readers' Theater is a text that has been written for readers to read aloud.

TEXT FOCUS

Directions tell how to do something step-by-step. As you read, pay attention to how dialogue is used to give directions. Tell how you can identify who is speaking in the play. When you write your own play, be sure to include the characters' names so the readers will know who is speaking.

 TEKS 2.8A identify/use dialogue in plays

Readers' Theater

Safety at Home

by Margaret Sweeny

Cast of Characters

Dad

Alexa

Jake

Dad: What did you do on your class trip?

Alexa: We visited an enormous fire station.

Jake: The fire chief gave a speech about fire safety.

Dad: I hope you were paying attention.

Alexa: We were. Later, we worked with a buddy to make a safety poster. I worked with Jake.

Jake: Look at our poster.

STOP, DROP, AND ROLL

1. If your clothes catch on fire, don't run.
2. STOP where you are.
3. DROP to the ground. Cover your face with your hands.
4. ROLL over and over to put out the fire.

Dad: I'm shocked! You know more about fire safety than I do.

Alexa: Everyone in our school obeys fire safety rules.

Jake: Guess what **get low and go** means?

Alexa: If the house is smoky, get low.

Jake: That's because smoke rises. Get low to stay below the smoke.

Alexa: Crawl to the nearest way out.

Jake: Then go to a safe meeting place to wait for your family.

Dad: Let's pick a meeting place right now!

Making Connections

 Text to Self TEKS RC-2(F)

Write a Caption Officer Buckle's safety tips are based on his own life. Think of a safety tip you learned. Draw a picture of what Gloria might do to act out that tip. Then write a caption for your picture.

 Text to Text TEKS RC-2(F), ELPS 4K

Compare and Contrast How are Officer Buckle's safety tips like the tips from *Safety at Home*? How are they different? Talk about it with a partner.

 Text to World TEKS 2.15A

Connect to Social Studies Gloria acted out safety tips, and Alexa and Jake made a fire safety poster. Think about some classroom safety tips. Make a poster for your classroom.

 TEKS 2.15A follow written directions; **RC-2(F)** make connections to experiences/texts/community; **ELPS 4K** employ analytical skills to demonstrate comprehension

Grammar

Abbreviations The names of days, months, and places are proper nouns that can be shortened. An **abbreviation** is a short way to write a word by taking out some of the letters and writing a period at the end.

Academic Language

abbreviation

Proper Nouns	Abbreviations
Monday	Mon.
March	Mar.
Main Street	Main St.

Write the proper noun for each abbreviation.

1 Nov.

2 Tues.

3 Elm Rd.

4 Canton St.

5 Jan.

6 Fri.

Conventions In your writing, make sure you write abbreviations correctly. Remember to use a period at the end of an abbreviation.

Incorrect	Correct
mr Wang says the police officer will visit our class on sept 4.	Mr. Wang says the police officer will visit our class on Sept. 4.

Connect Grammar to Writing

When you edit your persuasive essay, make sure you have used capital letters and end marks correctly.

Reading-Writing Workshop: Revise

Write to Persuade

✓ **Organization** When you write a **persuasive essay**, each reason can start a new paragraph.

Farah wrote a draft of her essay. Later, she moved things around so each reason started a new paragraph.

Writing Process Checklist

Prewrite

Draft

▶ **Revise**

☑ Did I tell my goal in a clear way?

☑ Did I give reasons for my goal?

☑ Did I include facts and examples for each reason?

☑ Did I sum up my reasons?

Edit

Publish and Share

Revised Draft

Our town library has a problem.
¶There are thirty-four people in
our town who read Braille. The
library has only twenty Braille
It needs more.
books.∧ It needs money for Braille
books. ¶Our school wants to do a
community project. Helping the
library would be a good one for us.

Help Our Library!

by Farah Jamali

Our town library has a problem. It needs money for Braille books.

There are thirty-four people in our town who read Braille. The library has only twenty Braille books. It needs more.

Our school is looking for a community project. Helping the library would be a good one for us. We could have a Read-a-thon to raise money for Braille books. Each student can fill out a pledge sheet.

> I started a new paragraph for each reason.

Reading as a Writer

How did Farah organize her essay to make her reasons clearer? How can you organize your reasons and details?

Read the selection. Then read each question. Choose the best answer for the question.

Koko the Talking Gorilla

1 Koko is an amazing gorilla. When she was one year old, she began to learn sign language. Her teachers wanted to see if she could learn to <u>communicate</u>. Today she knows more than one thousand signs! Koko can really talk using signs.

2 Koko has learned how to make jokes. She has even made up signs for words she had not been taught yet!

3 Once Koko asked if she could have a cat. Her teachers gave her one as a pet. The cat did not have a tail. So Koko named it All Ball. Koko is not only smart but funny, too!

GO ON ➔

1 Which word from the first paragraph means the same thing as the word <u>communicate</u>?

- ⬭ *talk*
- ⬭ *run*
- ⬭ *play*

2 The author probably wrote this to—

- ⬭ teach readers sign language
- ⬭ persuade people to have cats as pets
- ⬭ give facts about an interesting animal

3 Look at the following diagram of information from the article.

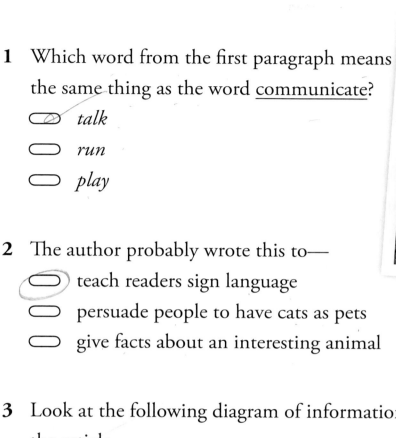

Which information belongs in the empty box?

- ⬭ Her cat did not have a tail.
- ⬭ She knows how to make jokes.
- ⬭ Her teacher bought a cat.

GO ON

Monkey Business

1   Helper monkeys are trained to <u>aid</u> people who cannot move their legs and arms. These small monkeys go to a special school. They learn how to help humans.

2   Helper monkeys can turn on lights or flip the pages of a book. They can open a refrigerator, take out a bottle of water, and put a straw in it. They even keep their human friends safe. They know how to get help when there is trouble.

1 What does the word <u>aid</u> mean in paragraph 1?

   ⬭ Try

   ⬭ Help

   ⬭ Stop

2 Why do helper monkeys go to a special school?

   ⬭ They learn how to talk.

   ⬭ They learn how to help people.

   ⬭ They learn how to write and draw.

3 The reader can tell that helper monkeys are—

   ⬭ large

   ⬭ loud

   ⬭ smart

STOP

TEKS 2.2H monitor decoding accuracy; **ELPS 2F** listen to/derive meaning from media; **3J** respond orally to information in media; **4F** use visual/contextual/peer/teacher support to read/comprehend texts; **4G** demonstrate comprehension through shared reading/retelling/responding/note-taking

Fluency

Read with a Recording   Listen to
one of the selections from this week
on a recording. Read along with the
recording to help you learn to say all
the words correctly. Then read without
the recording. Check that you are reading words
correctly and that all the words make sense. Listen
to the recording again if you need help.

Partner Reading   ELPS 4G

Work with a partner. Read pages 20–24 from
Henry and Mudge. As you read, pause and correct
any mistakes that you make in reading words.
Listen to your partner, and help him or her fix any
mistakes also. Read the pages again until you can
read without any mistakes. Then discuss with your
partner what the text was about.

TEKS 2.5D alphabetize/use dictionary/glossary; 2.29 share information/ideas by speaking clearly; **ELPS** 2H understand implicit ideas/information in spoken language; 3F ask/give information in various contexts; 3G express opinions/ideas/feelings; 3I adapt spoken language to purpose; 3H narrate/desribe/explain with detail

Vocabulary

Use a Glossary A glossary is a dictionary of important words found in a book. The words in the glossary are in alphabetical order like in a regular dictionary. Turn to the Glossary in your Student Book. Find the following:

- guide words on the first page of the glossary
- the meaning of the word *cousin*
- guide words to find the word *porch*
- the meaning of the word *visit*

Write your answers on a separate sheet of paper. Share your answers with a partner.

Listening and Speaking

What I Like to Do With My Family

Think of an activity you like to do with one or more members of your family. Examples include playing a game, visiting a special place, or cooking a favorite meal. Use these tips for speaking:

- Speak loudly so all of the listeners can hear you.
- Speak clearly and use complete sentences.
- Speak slowly so that your listeners understand everything that you say.

TEKS **2.2H** monitor decoding accuracy; **2.11** recognize literal/non-literal meanings of words/phrases

Fluency

Repeated Reading Reading a text several times will help you read all the words correctly.

1. Read pages 68–71 of *Henry and Mudge Under the Yellow Moon.*

2. Read the pages aloud quietly. Make sure you know how to say all the words. Pause and correct any mistakes you make. Focus on reading the words correctly.

3. Practice reading the pages until you can read them without making any mistakes.

Vocabulary

Find Word Meanings Sometimes words have different meanings. You can figure out the meanings of the words by using clues in the sentence and what you already know.

Read the sentences and the meanings under each sentence. Copy them onto a separate sheet of paper. For each sentence, circle the correct meaning for the underlined word in the sentence.

1. I had to <u>fly</u> through my breakfast so I didn't miss the school bus.
   a. hurry   b. go into the air

2. Our team had a <u>rocky</u> start in the game because we made a lot of mistakes.
   a. difficult   b. full of stones

TEKS 2.2G identify/read high-frequency words; **ELPS** 3B expand/internalize initial English vocabulary

High-Frequency Words

Identify Words   Work with a partner to read and identify the words below.

- Copy the words onto cards.

- Spread the cards out in front of you.

- Read them together.

- One partner should call out a word while the other partner holds up the matching card. Switch roles.

today   those   places   bring

cheer   until   hundred   read

mind   could

TEKS 2.2G identify/read high-frequency words; **ELPS** 3B expand/internalize initial English vocabulary

High-Frequency Words

Identify and Sort Words   Work with a partner. Read aloud the words below together. Then one partner should point to a word and the other partner should read it aloud. Switch roles.

green	eat	says
table	long	city
walked	school	find
cold	play	little

On a separate sheet of paper, make a chart like the one below. With your partner, sort the words into groups. Then read aloud the words.

Words That Name Something	Words That Describe Something	Action Words

TEKS 2.2D read words with prefixes/suffixes; 2.5A use prefixes/suffixes to determine meaning; ELPS 4A learn English sound-letter relationships/decode

Vocabulary

Identify the Prefix   Read the prefixes in the box.

> mis-   re-   un-

Number a sheet of paper 1–6. For each sentence below, choose the prefix from the box to complete the word. Write each sentence with the new word. Make sure the sentence makes sense with the new word. Tell what the word with the prefix means.

1. The beaver _____fills cracks between the logs in its lodge.

2. Without a home, animals would be _____safe from predators.

3. Some birds _____build homes made by others.

4. Gophers make burrows so they will not _____place their food or offspring.

5. The animals' homes are _____like in many ways.

6. Animals work hard to build their homes, so they do not _____treat them.

489

TEKS **2.2H** monitor decoding accuracy; **2.3C** establish purpose/monitor comprehension; **ELPS 4F** use visual/contextual/peer/teacher support to read/comprehend texts; **4G** demonstrate comprehension through shared reading/retelling/responding/note-taking

Fluency

Partner Reading   When you read, make sure that you read words correctly. This will help you understand what you read.

1. Work with a partner. Take turns reading aloud pages 200–205 from *The Ugly Vegetables.*

2. As you read, check that you read words correctly and that the words make sense.

3. As you read, think about the ideas in the story. Ask yourself questions such as "Does this make sense?" Go back and reread if you don't understand something you read.

4. Give your partner feedback on his or her reading. Talk about what you read. Tell each other what it was about.

TEKS 2.2G identify/read high-frequency words; **ELPS** 3B expand/internalize initial English vocabulary

High-Frequency Words

Identify Words   Work with a partner to read and identify the words below. Then you and your partner should each make a set of the word cards. One partner should read a word. The other partner should hold up the matching word card from his or her set. Continue for all words. Then switch roles.

pictures   told   try   second

window   know   funny   most

while   air

TEKS **2.29** share information/ideas by speaking clearly; **2.30** follow discussion rules; **ELPS 2H** understand implicit ideas/information in spoken language; **3C** speak using a variety of grammatical structures; **3F** ask/give information in various contexts

Listening and Speaking

All About Storms Think about one of the storms described in *Super Storms*. On a separate sheet of paper, make a web like the one below. Put the name of the storm in the center oval. Put facts about the storm in the other ovals.

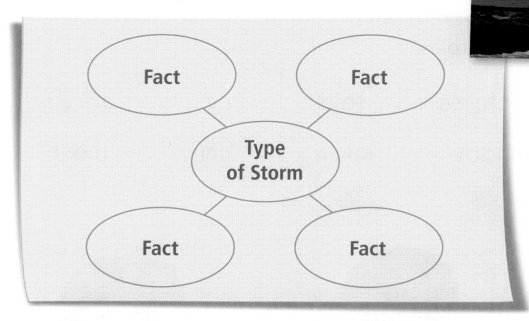

Find a partner who has chosen a different storm than you. Tell your partner about the storm. Follow these tips for listening and speaking:

- Speak clearly and slowly.

- Speak in complete sentences.

- Stay on the topic.

- Listen carefully. When the speaker is done, ask questions if you didn't understand something.

492

TEKS 2.2A(i) decode using single letters; 2.2A(ii) decode words with consonant blends ELPS 4A learn English sound-letter relationships/decode

Phonics

Sort Endings   With a partner, read each word in the box. On a separate sheet of paper, make a chart like the one below. Sort the words in the box by endings. Then say a sentence using each of the words.

| spilled | standing | riding |
| bringing | jumped | raced |

-ed	-ing

Write Endings

On a separate sheet of paper, copy the words below in a list. Read each word and write it with an *-ed* ending and an *-ing* ending. Then read the new words.

1. close

2. want

3. ask

4. spike

5. turn

6. start

TEKS 2.5C identify/use antonyms/synonyms

Vocabulary

Same Meaning   A synonym is a word that means the same or nearly the same as another word. On a separate sheet of paper, copy these words from *How Chipmunk Got His Stripes.* Write a synonym for each one. Then work with a partner to write the synonyms in sentences.

1. **biggest**

2. **said**

3. **little**

4. **happy**

5. **grabbed**

6. **idea**

TEKS 2.6B compare folktale variants

Comprehension

How Armadillo Got Short Ears

Young Coyote loved to brag. One day at recess Coyote said, "I bet that I can howl so loudly that even the moon can hear me."

"Oh, really?" replied Armadillo. "Try to howl at the moon tonight. Ask it to tell us why it changes shape. With my long ears, I'll surely be able to hear what the moon says."

"No problem!" replied Coyote. He sent a text message to all his friends telling them to come hear him howl at the moon.

All of the animals came that night. Coyote howled and howled, but the moon didn't reply.

"Ha, ha!" laughed Armadillo. "The moon can't hear you!"

495

TEKS 2.6B compare folktale variants

"Stop laughing at me!" cried the embarrassed Coyote. He pinned Armadillo down by his long ears.

"Oh, wait," said Armadillo. His ears hurt a lot, but he didn't want Coyote to think he was weak. "I think I hear the moon," Armadillo said slyly. "Let go of my ears so I can hear better."

Coyote loosened his grip a little. Armadillo scooted out from under him and ran away. When he got home, he was surprised to see that his ears were very short. He felt bad for teasing Coyote, but his ears never grew long again.

Even with his short ears, though, Armadillo can sometimes hear Coyote howling at the moon.

Settings and Plots

TEKS 2.6B

Look back at *How Chipmunk Got His Stripes* on page 259. Compare it to *How Armadillo Got Short Ears*. How are the settings alike? How are they different? Think about the plots. How are they alike? How are they different?

TEKS 2.2B(i) decode words with closed syllables; 2.2B(ii) decode words with open syllables, 2.2B(iv) decode words with VCe pattern

Phonics

Syllable Patterns   Use what you know about syllables to read aloud the words in Column A below to a partner. Write the words on a sheet of paper and draw a line between the syllables. Then have your partner repeat for Column B.

Column A	Column B
chipmunk	mistake
frozen	zebra
contest	napkin
kitten	picnic
inside	decide
hotel	relax
problem	nutmeg

TEKS 2.2F identify/read contractions; 2.5A use prefixes/suffixes to determine meaning; **ELPS** 4A learn English sound-letter relationships/ decode

Phonics

All About Contractions   A contraction is a shortened way of saying and writing one or more words. Use an apostrophe (') to take the place of missing letters.

- Look for contractions on pages 296–298 of *Jellies*.

- Write the words and read them aloud.

- Then write the two words that make up the contraction.

Vocabulary

Identify the Suffix   Read each sentence below. Use the suffix *-ful* or *-less* to complete each word. Then read the new word and tell its meaning. Then read the whole sentence.

1. Dangerous jellyfish have a power____ sting.

2. Without a brain, jellyfish are power____ to decide what to eat.

3. Fish should be care____ not to swim around jellyfish.

4. Jellyfish can be harm____.

5. If a jellyfish makes a care____ mistake, it might be food for a sea turtle.

TEKS 2.12 read independently/paraphrase; **ELPS** 2I demonstrate listening comprehension of spoken English; **3B** expand/internalize initial English vocabulary; **3E** share information in cooperative learning interactions

Independent Reading

Choose a Book When you choose a book to read, think about the questions below to help you make a good choice.

- **Purpose**—What is your reason for reading? Is it to be entertained or to get information?

- **Topic**—What subject do you want to read about?

- **Genre**—Do you want to read fiction, nonfiction, or poetry?

- **Author**—Do you have a favorite author or series of books you like to read?

- **Difficulty**—Is the book too easy, too hard, or just right?

Have a Book Talk

After you read, have a book talk with a small group of classmates. Follow these steps:

- Show the book's cover and a few pictures or photos.
- Tell about the book in your own words.
- Look at everyone and speak loudly.
- As you listen to classmates' book talks, write the title of each book and a few notes about the book.

TEKS 2.2A(i) decode using single letters; 2.2a(iii) decode words with consonant digraphs; 2.5A use prefixes/suffixes to determine meaning; **ELPS** 4A learn English sound-letter relationships/decode

Phonics

Add –s or –es   Copy the chart below on a separate sheet of paper. Read the base word. Write the base word and the correct ending. Then read the new word.

Base Words	Base Words + -s or -es
take	
dress	
know	
become	
watch	
point	

-s

-es

Vocabulary

Add a Prefix   On a separate sheet of paper, write one of the following prefixes to complete each statement: *re-, un-,* or *mis-.* Read each word aloud.

_____ + pack = to pack again

_____ + healthy = not healthy

_____ + understand = to understand badly

_____ + write = to write again

_____ + true = not true

TEKS 2.9A compare several works by same author

Comprehension

Compare and Contrast Story Endings Think about the end of the plot in *Henry and Mudge* and in *Henry and Mudge Under the Yellow Moon*. Read **Student Book** pages 23–24 and pages 75–76 again to help you remember the ending of each story. With a partner, list ways that the end of each story's plot is the same. Then list ways that the two plot endings are different.

TEKS 2.9A compare several works by same author

Comprehension

Write About Settings   Sometimes an author will give clues to help you make an inference about the setting of a story. Look at the words and illustrations on **Student Book** page 96, *Diary of a Spider*, and on page 328 of *Click, Clack, Moo: Cows That Type*. Both stories are written by Doreen Cronin.

How is the setting on page 96 the same as the setting on page 328? How are the settings on those pages different? What clues does the author give to help you figure out the settings? Write a few sentences to explain your ideas.

TEKS **2.2A(i)** decode using single letters; **2.2A(iv)** decode using vowel digraphs/diphthongs; **ELPS 2B** recognize elements of the English sound system; **4A** learn English sound-letter relationships/decode

Phonics

Guess the Word   Work with a partner. Read the words below. Then write them on word cards. Place the cards facedown in a pile.

pay	fail	sail	crayons
mail	tray	raisin	painting
play	away		

Take turns choosing a card and giving clues to help your partner guess the word. Continue until all of the word cards have been used.

TEKS 2.2F identify/read contractions

Phonics

What Am I? On a separate sheet of paper, write the contractions to complete the sentences. Use the words after the sentence to help you. Read the sentences aloud. Then draw a picture of the animal that is talking.

1. _____ got four legs and fur. (I have)

2. _____ hard for me to keep my tail still when _____ happy. (It is) (I am)

3. _____ run and play together. (Let us)

4. _____ have so much fun. (We will)

TEKS 2.2H monitor decoding accuracy; **2.3C** establish purpose/monitor comprehension; **ELPS 2B** recognize elements of the English sound system; **4A** learn English sound-letter relationships/decode

Phonics

Rhyme Time   On a separate sheet of paper, write the word that fits each clue below. Then with a partner, say and write three rhyming words. Underline the *ee* or *ea* in each word.

1. **This is what you do when you are tired.**

   <u>swee</u>p   sleep   sweat

2. **This is something true or alive.**

   real   read   red

3. **This is what crackers are made from.**

   <u>wha</u>le   <u>whea</u>t   wheel

4. **This is a part of the leg that bends.**

   kn<u>ow</u>   kn<u>ea</u>d   kn<u>ee</u>

Fluency

Partner Reading   With a partner, read aloud the poems on pages 405-406. Practice reading the important words a little louder than the other words. As you read, check that you and your partner are reading the words correctly. Then take turns reading each poem aloud by yourself. Talk about what each poem was about. Tell something that you liked about each poem.

TEKS 2.2F identify/read contractions; 2.5D alphabetize/use dictionary/glossary; **ELPS** 4C develop/comprehend basic English vocabulary and structures

Vocabulary

Word Meanings   Use a dictionary to find what a word means and how to spell it. Reread pages 390–391 in *Schools Around the World*. Look for these words:

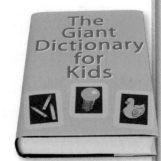

climate   resources   materials

travel   depends

Use a dictionary to find the correct meaning of each word. Write the definition for each word. Check that the meaning is the same as what the word means in *Schools Around the World*. Then write each word in a new sentence.

Phonics

Find the Contractions   Read the sentences. Look for the contractions. Read each one aloud. Write the two words that make up the contraction.

Today's the day the artist comes to our school.

We're having an art show for him.

We've all made works of art.

I've made something out of clay.

It's a four-legged animal!

Our teacher says, "Let's get everything ready. He'll be here soon."

TEKS 2.5A use prefixes/suffixes to determine meaning; **ELPS** 2A distinguish sounds/intonation patterns of English; 2B recognize elements of the English sound system

Phonics

Build Words Add *oa* and *ow* to complete each word below. Write the word on paper and read it aloud. Then use the words in sentences.

b _ _ t	s h a d _ _	f o l l _ _
c _ _ t	g r _ _	f l _ _ t
g l _ _	l _ _	s _ _ p

Vocabulary

Add a Suffix Read each sentence and the words below it. Complete the sentence with a word that means the same as the words below the sentence and ends with *-ly*. Reread each sentence.

1. Mom likes music, so she sings _____.
   (in a glad way)

2. She is careful to sing each note _____.
   (in a correct way)

3. I watched _____ as she sang for my class.
   (in a way that is proud)

4. Sometimes we sing in the car _____.
   (in a loud way)

5. At bedtime, she sings to me _____.
   (in a way that is soft)

507

TEKS 2.2A(i) decode using single letters; 2.2A(ii) decode using consonant blends; 2.2A(iii) decode using consonant digraphs; 2.2A(iv) decode words using vowel digraphs/diphthongs

Phonics

Compound words   Sometimes two words put together can make a new word. These words are called compound words. Read the words in both columns below. Then choose a word from the left that can be joined with a word on the right to make a compound word. Write the compound words and read them aloud.

sun	child
butter	shine
rain	place
grand	end
week	fly
fire	drops

TEKS **2.2H** monitor decoding accuracy; **ELPS** **4F** use visual/contextual/peer/teacher support to read/comprehend texts; **4G** demonstrate comprehension through shared reading/retelling/responding/note-taking

Fluency

Repeated Reading

Reading a story several times will help you say all the words correctly.

1. With a partner, read aloud pages 448–455 of *Officer Buckle and Gloria*.

2. If you make a mistake, go back and reread the sentence. Make sure the sentences make sense.

3. Give your partner feedback on his or her reading. Help each other read words correctly and to understand what you read.

4. Practice reading the pages until you can read them without making any mistakes.

TEKS 2.5D alphabetize/use dictionary/glossary

Vocabulary

Use a Dictionary   You can use a dictionary to find what a word means and how to spell it. A dictionary lists words in alphabetical order.

Reread pages 449–454 in *Officer Buckle and Gloria*. Look for these words.

| tips | swivel | commands | popped | roared |

Write the words in alphabetical order. Then use a dictionary to find the correct meaning for each word. On a separate sheet of paper, write each word and its definition. Be sure that the meaning that you write is the same as the meaning of the word in the story. Then write a new sentence for each word. Share your sentences with a partner.

The Giant Dictionary for Kids

TEKS 2.2E identify/read abbreviations

Grammar

What's the Correct Abbreviation?   Abbreviations are short forms of longer words. They start with a capital letter and end with a period.

On a separate sheet of paper, write the correct abbreviation for each word.

1. **Wednesday**   3. **August**   5. **January**
2. **Sunday**   4. **December**   6. **Thursday**

Rewrite each item correctly.

7. **mrs toppel**   9. **tues, nov 18**   11. **dr dean**
8. **mr jones**   10. **fri, sept 30**   12. **ms burnett**

TEKS 2.2B(i) decode words with closed syllables; 2.2B(ii) decode words with open syllables, 2.2B(iv) decode words with VCe pattern; 2.2B(vi) decode words with vowel digraphs/diphthongs syllabication patterns

Phonics

Syllable Patterns   Use what you know about syllables to read aloud the words in Column A below to a partner. Write the words on a sheet of paper and draw a line between the syllables. Then have your partner repeat for Column B.

Column A	Column B
even	mistake
muffin	velvet
invite	bracelet
crayon	painting
decrease	open
peeking	leaking
between	delay

in vite

Glossary

This glossary can help you find the meanings of some of the words in this book. The meanings given are the meanings of the words as they are used in the book. Sometimes a second meaning is also given.

A

alone

Without anyone or anything: *Sometimes she liked to be* **alone** *in the tree house and read stories.*

attend

To look carefully at or take care of: *We try to* **attend** *to the work we are asked to do.*

attention

A form of **attend**: *When someone read a story to them, their* **attention** *was very good.*

B

beak

A bill, or the hard mouth parts of a bird: *The baby birds opened their* **beaks** *wide, waiting for their food.*

behave

To act in a certain way: *We always tried to* **behave** *well when visitors were in the room.*

behavior

A form of **behave**: *His* **behavior** *in school was better than it was at home.*

believe

To accept as true or real: *I* **believe** *that you have the hat.*

bend

To become curved or not straight: *The tree branches* **bend** *down in the heavy snow.*

beak

beware

To be careful or look out for a problem: *The sign told us to* ***beware*** *of falling rocks.*

bloom

To blossom or grow into flower: *Some plants* ***bloom*** *in the spring, while others are just starting to grow.*

bloom

blooming

A form of **bloom**: *Butterflies come to the garden when that bush is* ***blooming***.

brag

To boast, or speak with too much pride: *She tries not to* ***brag*** *about winning, but she wants us to know.*

branch

A part that grows out from a trunk of a tree: *All the* ***branches*** *of the tree had yellow leaves.*

break

To separate into pieces or tear apart: *We had to* ***break*** *the ground up with different garden tools.*

breeze

A light wind: *The puppy smelled smoke when she sniffed the* ***breeze***.

buddy

A pal or close friend: *He became my* ***buddy*** *during our first summer in camp.*

burst

To be full to the point of breaking open: *She tried hard not to* ***burst*** *out laughing when she saw the silly hat.*

bursting

A form of **burst**: *The milkweed pod was **bursting** with silky seeds.*

bursting

busy

To be actively at work: *The **busy** squirrel gathered nuts.*

C

chipmunk

An animal that looks similar to a squirrel but is smaller and has a striped back: *Three brown **chipmunks** chased each other up the tree in our backyard.*

choice

The act of choosing or the chance to choose: *We had many **choices** about what to see in the city.*

collar

A leather, cloth, or metal band for an animal's neck: *Both of our dogs wear red **collars** around their necks.*

community

A group of people who live together in the same area: *Our **community** is filled with friendly neighbors.*

cousin

A child of one's aunt or uncle: *My **cousin** stayed with us for two days.*

crown

A head covering that a queen, king, or other ruler might wear: *She used paper, glue, and glitter to make a **crown** for her costume.*

crown

culture

The traditions, arts, and beliefs of a certain group of people: *In his Native American **culture**, the fall harvest is a time for celebration.*

curious

Eager to find out or learn about something: *He was **curious** about many kinds of sea animals, so he loved the aquarium.*

curl

To make a rounded shape: *He showed us how to **curl** slices of carrot in cold water.*

curled

A form of **curl**: *The kitten **curled** up in his lap and purred happily.*

curly

A form of **curl**: *My brother's hair is so thick and **curly** he can hardly comb it.*

D

damage

To harm or injure: *The flood might **damage** the bridge so that it must be closed for repair.*

danger

The chance of harm, or something that may cause harm: *We had good reasons to worry about **danger** deep in the dark cave.*

dangerous

A form of **danger**: *The little rabbit knew it was a **dangerous** place, but she hopped closer.*

dark

Without light or with very little light: *With no moon, the night was **dark**.*

darkness

A form of **dark**: *In the **darkness**, he couldn't tell what kind of animal was outside.*

decide

To make up one's mind: *Tomorrow I will **decide** what to do about the party.*

deep

Located far below the surface or far from an opening: *They buried the treasure **deep** in the ground near a pine tree.*

deepest

A form of **deep**: *In the **deepest** part of the ocean, it is very dark.*

demand

To ask firmly or to require: *The teachers in that school **demand** hard work from their students.*

direction

The place or line along which someone or something goes: *Walk in the **direction** of the town.*

direction

disgust

To cause a sick or bad feeling: *If those movies **disgust** you, please stop watching them.*

disgusting

A form of **disgust**: *When she sniffed at the garbage pail, it smelled **disgusting**.*

drift

To float along or be carried along on water or air: *Our raft will **drift** if we do not paddle.*

G5

drool

To let saliva drip from the mouth: *My baby sister **drools** on my arm and makes my sleeve wet.*

drooled

A form of **drool**: *He **drooled** when he looked at all the delicious food.*

E

enormous

Huge, or very large in size: *Hank was an **enormous** dog, almost the size of a cow.*

enormous

equal

To be the same as: *Seven days **equal** one week, and twenty-four hours equal one day.*

F

flash

To give out a sudden bright light: *The fireworks **flash** in the night sky, and people cheer.*

flash

flop

To drop or hang heavily: *When I'm really tired, I **flop** onto the couch for a nap.*

floppy

A form of flop: *Some rabbits have **floppy** ears that droop around their face.*

furious

Full of great anger, or raging: *She was so **furious** that she threw a pillow across the room.*

G

gather

To bring or come together in one place: *We will **gather** for the meeting at noon today.*

gathered

A form of **gather**: *After the whole group **gathered** on stage, they began to sing.*

grew

A form of **grow**: *My dad **grew** a big, thick beard that almost covered his face!*

grow

To get bigger, increase, or spread: *That little patch of flowers is starting to **grow** across the whole yard.*

H

hang

To be attached at the upper end: *Many colorful paintings **hang** on the walls of the museum.*

heal

To get better or become well: *Most cuts **heal** quickly if you take care of them.*

healed

A form of **heal**: *When the deer's leg **healed**, she ran as fast as ever.*

height

The distance from bottom to top: *The **height** of the mountain is about a mile above sea level.*

height

G7

hour

A unit of time that equals sixty minutes: *They spent many* **hours** *playing games at camp.*

I

ill

Sick or not healthy: *They have been* **ill** *with the flu.*

illness

A form of **ill**: *After an* **illness**, *people may feel tired for a few days.*

imitate

To copy the actions, looks, or sounds of: *Little children* **imitate** *their parents or older children in their family.*

imitated

A form of **imitate**: *After I* **imitated** *the steps many times, I learned to do the dance.*

impatient

Not able or willing to wait: *She walked because she was too* **impatient** *to wait for the bus.*

impossible

Not possible or not able to happen: *It will be* **impossible** *to finish on time unless you start now.*

inform

To tell about something: *The guide* **informs** *people about animals on the nature trail.*

insect

A bug that has six legs, a body with three main parts, and, usually, wings: *She liked to watch* **insects** *at the pond.*

insect

J

judge

To listen or look at in order to decide about: *At the fair, it was fun to judge which pie should win the first prize.*

K

know

To understand or have the facts about: *Do you know what causes thunder?*

knowledge

Facts and ideas, or information: *Their teacher had knowledge about many subjects, such as weather and history.*

L

language

A system of words, expressions, signs, or symbols shared by a group of people. At our house we speak two *languages: Spanish and English.*

lesson

Something to be learned or taught: *After a few more lessons, I'll be able to skate like an Olympic athlete!*

M

millions

A very large number, or more than a thousand thousands: *There are millions of fish in the sea.*

motion

Movement, gesture, or the act of moving: *The motion of the boat on the waves made him feel sleepy.*

muscle

Body tissue that helps many different parts of the body move and work: *Our muscles will get stronger from all the exercise we do.*

museum

A building where art or other important things are displayed, or shown: *The **museum** he liked best had many buttons to press and things to do.*

N

nod

To move the head down and up in a quick motion that may mean "okay": *You will be out of the game if you move before I **nod** my head.*

nodded

A form of **nod**: *I was glad when my father **nodded** to let us know we could go.*

noise

A sound that may be loud or unpleasant: *You could tell from the **noises** that there were many animals in the barn.*

notice

To pay attention to or make note of: *I sat in the back and hoped that nobody would **notice** me.*

noise

noticed

A form of **notice**: *The first thing he **noticed** was how fast the clouds moved across the sky.*

nursery

A room for babies or young children: *He remembered playing happily in the **nursery**.*

O

obey

To do what is asked: *After training, the horse **obeys** the rider.*

P

piano

A musical instrument with a keyboard: *She could play tunes on the piano.*

piano

pick

Gather: *If you pick some wildflowers, I'll put them in a vase for Aunt Mimi.*

picked

A form of **pick**: *We picked enough berries from our garden to make twelve pies!*

plain

Not fancy or pretty: *The plants look plain before they bloom.*

pond

A small body of water in the shape of a lake or pool: *Frogs sat at the edge of the pond.*

porch

A structure with a roof that is attached to the outside of a house: *They kept two chairs and a low table on the porch.*

pound

To hammer or hit hard again and again: *When you pound on the drum, I want to leave the room.*

pounding

A form of **pound**: *The pounding rain on the tent kept her from falling asleep.*

prevent

To stop or keep from happening: *You can prevent fires by being careful.*

problem

Something that is difficult to deal with or understand: *The group tried to solve the* ***problem*** *by talking together.*

Q

quiet

Silent, calm, or with hardly any sound: *The house was finally* ***quiet*** *after all the children were asleep.*

R

reach

To get to or go as far as: *When all the boats* ***reach*** *the shore, I will feel better.*

real

Not imagined or made up: *She wanted to have a* ***real*** *pet and not just a toy animal.*

remember

To think of again or bring back in the mind: *I* ***remember*** *the first word I learned to read.*

remembered

A form of **remember**: *He always* ***remembered*** *his grandpa's stories.*

rotten

Decayed or spoiled: *Some insects eat* ***rotten*** *fruit that people throw away.*

row

In a line or in sequence, one after another: *I got an A on two tests in a* ***row***, *which is a new record for me!*

S

safe

Free from danger or harm: *The mother bird saw that her babies were* ***safe*** *in the nest.*

safe

safety

A form of **safe**: *Most playground rules were made for your **safety**.*

scare

To frighten or make afraid: *This dragon mask might **scare** some little children.*

scent

A special smell that comes from something: *The **scent** of roses reminded her of her grandmother's yard in the spring.*

scent

scream

To make a long, loud, high-pitched cry: *When my little sister **screams**, I hold my ears.*

screaming

A form of **scream**: *When the game got close, many people started **screaming** for their team to win.*

shake

To move quickly up and down or back and forth: *He sometimes will **shake** the toy bank to hear the coins inside.*

shape

To give a certain form or shape to: *I **shape** the clay to look like woodland animals.*

shaped

A form of **shape**: *The sign at the farm stand was large and **shaped** like a pumpkin.*

share

To divide with others or take part in: *Let's **share** this last orange.*

shock

To surprise or greatly upset: *The news will **shock** you, so please sit down.*

shocked

A form of **shock**: *I was **shocked** when I found that the jewels were missing.*

shovel

A tool with a long handle and a flattened scoop: *The man is using a snow **shovel**.*

shovel

silence

A form of **silent**: *The **silence** in the library helps people enjoy their reading.*

silent

Quiet, making or having no sound: *The room was **silent**, so she thought everyone had gone.*

simple

Easy, or not complicated: *The directions on the box looked **simple**, and she followed them carefully.*

smooth

Going along evenly, or without rough parts: *The custard was **smooth** and made her sore throat feel better.*

south

The direction to the left of a person who faces the sunset: *My grandparents go **south** each winter to bask in the warm weather.*

special

Different from what is common or usual: *Birthdays are **special** occasions.*

speech

The act of speaking, or a talk: *She practiced at home before she gave the **speech** in class.*

spend

To cause or allow time to pass: *We will **spend** the day at the beach.*

sprinkle

To scatter in drops or small pieces: *We always **sprinkle** salt into the water before it boils.*

sprinkled

A form of **sprinkle**: *The children **sprinkled** fish food into the goldfish bowl.*

stand

To be a certain height: *Medium-size dogs usually **stand** between two and three feet tall.*

station

A place where a special service is provided: *We got our tickets and waited at the train **station**.*

station

stick

To attach or to keep in one place: *We **stick** a stamp on each card before we mail it.*

sticky

Holding together as with glue or hard to pull apart: *After eating the honey, they licked their **sticky** fingers.*

stood

A form of **stand**: *Last year my sister stood three feet tall, but now she's almost four feet.*

straight

Not curving, curling, or bending: *My hair is straight and never gets wavy.*

stuck

A form of **stick**: *The truck got stuck in the heavy snow.*

subject

Course of study: *Science and social studies are his favorite subjects in school.*

sudden

Happening or coming without warning: *On the hike, we were caught in a sudden storm.*

suddenly

A form of **sudden**: *The birds flew away as suddenly as they had landed in the yard.*

T

tease

To make fun of or try to bother: *My friends used to tease me about my hair.*

top

The highest or upper part: *The tops of those mountains are covered in snow.*

tough

Strong and not likely to break or wear out: *The hiking boots were warm and tough, so he could walk outdoors in any weather.*

toward

In the direction of: *We walked toward the tower and watched for a light.*

transportation

Means of getting from one place to another: *Trains are my favorite kind of transportation.*

tunnel

A passage underground or underwater: *The train passed through the **tunnel** to the other side of the mountain.*

tunnel

turn

Transform; change: *When the skies **turn** from blue to gray, a storm is on the way.*

turned

A form of **turn**: *The weather **turned** colder as soon as the calendar said fall.*

U

understand

To get the meaning of: *I **understand** the meaning of a few Spanish words.*

V

visit

To go or come to see: *We will **visit** our friends in the city.*

W

weak

Having little or no power, strength, or energy: *The battery was so **weak** that our flashlight didn't help much.*

weaker

A form of **weak**: *She was **weaker** after being sick, but then she grew stronger.*

wear

To have on the body: *In cold places, people **wear** two or three layers of clothes.*

G17

weigh

Find out the weight or heaviness of: *The doctor will* **weigh** *you on a scale before your checkup.*

weighed

A form of weigh: *I* **weighed** *my dog three times to make sure she was really that heavy!*

whenever

At whatever time: **Whenever** *it rains, my cat wants to come inside.*

wind

To move along with twists and turns: *We* **wind** *the string around the stick to bring the kite back in.*

winding

A form of **wind**: *They followed a* **winding** *path higher and higher up the mountain.*

winding

wonder

A marvel or something amazing: *Their tricks on the high wire were a* **wonder** *to everyone who watched.*

wonderful

A form of **wonder**: *Their day at the beach was* **wonderful** *from beginning to end.*

woods

Forest: *Rashid walked quietly through the* **woods**, *looking for birds in the trees.*

wrap

To cover by winding or folding: ***Wrap*** *a scarf around your neck before you go out in the cold wind.*

wrapped

A form of **wrap**: *We* ***wrapped*** *our sandwiches in foil for the picnic.*

wrapped

wrinkle

To form small, uneven lines or creases: *This cloth will* ***wrinkle*** *after you wash it, so you need an iron.*

wrinkled

A form of **wrinkle**: *The shirt was* ***wrinkled***, *so she tried to smooth it out.*

Acknowledgments

Main Literature Selections

"Abuelita's Lap" from *Confetti: Poems for Children*, by Pat Mora. Text copyright © 1996 by Pat Mora. Reprinted by permission of Lee & Low Books, Inc.

Animals Building Homes by Wendy Perkins. Copyright © 2004 by Capstone Press. All rights reserved. Reprinted by permission of Capstone Press Publishers.

"The Best" from *Did You See What I Saw?* by Kay Winters. Copyright © 1996 by Kay Winters. Reprinted by permission of Viking Penguin, A Division of Penguin Young Readers Group, A Member of Penguin Group (USA) Inc. All rights reserved.

Click, Clack, Moo: Cows That Type by Doreen Cronin, illustrated by Betsy Lewin. Text copyright © 2000 by Doreen Cronin. Illustrations copyright © 2000 by Betsy Lewin. Reprinted by permission of Simon & Schuster's Books for Young Readers, an Imprint of Simon & Schuster's Children's Publishing Division. All rights reserved.

Diary of a Spider by Doreen Cronin, illustrated by Harry Bliss. Text copyright © 2005 by Doreen Cronin. Illustrations copyright © 2005 by Harry Bliss. Reprinted by permission of HarperCollins Children's Books, a division of HarperCollins Publishers, and Pippin Properties, Inc.

"Everybody Says" from *Everything and Anything* by Dorothy Aldis, copyright © 1925-1927, renewed 1953-1955 by Dorothy Aldis. Reprinted by permission of G.P. Putnam's Sons, A Division of Penguin Young Readers Group, A Member of Penguin Group (USA) Inc. All rights reserved.

Henry and Mudge: The First Book by Cynthia Rylant, illustrated by Suçie Stevenson. Text copyright © 1987 by Cynthia Rylant. Illustrations copyright © 1997 by Suçie Stevenson. Reprinted by permission of Simon & Schuster's Books for Young Readers, an imprint of Simon & Schuster Children's Publishing Division. All rights reserved.

Henry and Mudge Under the Yellow Moon by Cynthia Rylant, illustrated by Suçie Stevenson. Text copyright © 1987 by Cynthia Rylant. Illustrations copyright © 1997 by Suçie Stevenson. Reprinted by permission of Simon & Schuster Children's Publishing Division. All rights reserved.

How Chipmunk Got His Stripes by Joseph and James Bruchac, illustrated by José Aruego & Ariane Dewey. Text copyright © 2001 by Joseph Bruchac and James Bruchac. Illustrations copyright © 2001 by José Aruego and Ariane Dewey. All rights reserved. Published by permission of Dial Books for Young Readers, a member of Penguin Books for Young Readers, a division of Penguin Group (USA) Inc.

"I Have To Write A Poem For Class" from *What A Day It Was At School!* by Jack Prelutsky. Copyright © 2006 by Jack Prelutsky. Reprinted by permission of HarperCollins Publishers.

Jellies: The Life of Jellyfish by Twig C. George. Text copyright © 2000 by Twig C. George. All rights reserved. Reprinted by permission of Millbrook Press, a division of Lerner Publishing Group, and Curtis Brown, Ltd.

Mi Familia/My Family by George Ancona, children's drawings by Camila Carballo, photographs by George Ancona. Text copyright © 2004 by George Ancona. Children's drawings copyright © 2004 by Camila Carballo. Photographs copyright © 2004 by George Ancona. All rights reserved. Reprinted by permission of Children's Press, an imprint of Scholastic Library Publishing, Inc.

"Morning Sun" from *Laughing Tomatoes and Other Spring Poems* by Francisco X. Alarcón. Copyright © 1997 by Francisco X. Alarcón. Reprinted by permission of the publisher, Children's Book Press, San Francisco, CA, www.childrensbookpress.org.

Officer Buckle and Gloria written and illustrated by Peggy Rathmann. Text and illustrations copyright © 1995 by Peggy Rathmann. All rights reserved. Reprinted by permission of G. P. Putnam's Sons, a division of Penguin Putnam Books for Young Readers, a division of Penguin Group (USA) Inc., and Sheldon Fogelman Agency, Inc.

"Rain" by Shisei-Jo from *Japanese Haiku*, translated by Peter Beilenson. Copyright © 1955-56 by Peter Pauper Press. Reprinted by permission of Peter Pauper Press.

"School" from *Hello School!: A Room Full of Poems* by Dee Lillegard, illustrated by Don Carter. Copyright © 2001 by Dee Lillegard. Reprinted by permission of Alfred A. Knopf, an imprint of Random House Children's Books, a division of Random House, Inc., and BookStop Literary Agency, LLC.

Schools Around the World by Margaret C. Hall. Originally published as Schools. Text copyright © 2002 Heinemann Library. Reprinted by permission of Heinemann Library, a division of Pearson Education.

Super Storms by Seymour Simon. Text copyright © 2002 by Seymour Simon. All rights reserved. Reprinted by permission of Chronicle Books, LLC, San Francisco, California, USA.

Teacher's Pets by Dale Ann Dodds, illustrated by Marilyn Hafner. Text copyright © 2006 by Dale Ann Dodds. Illustrations copyright © 2006 by Marilyn Hafner. Reprinted by permission of the publisher, Candlewick Press Inc.

The Ugly Vegetables written and illustrated by Grace Lin. Text and illustrations copyright © 1999 by Grace Lin. All rights reserved. Reprinted by permission of Charlesbridge Publishing, Inc.

Excerpt from "What is a family?" from *Fathers, Mothers, Sisters, Brothers: A Collection of Family Poems* by Mary Ann Hoberman. Copyright © 1991 Mary Ann Hoberman. Reprinted by permission of Little Brown & Company and Gina Maccoby Literary Agency.

Credits

Photo Credits

Placement Key: (t) top; (b) bottom; (l) left; (r) right; (c) center; (bg) background; (fg) foreground; (i) inset.

8a Andy Sacks/Getty Images; **8b** Andy Sacks/Getty Images; **9** Andy Sacks/Getty Images; **10** (tl) Arco Images GmbH/Alamy; (tr) © Jeffy Shulman/SuperStock; **11** (tl) Sean MacLeay/Shutterstock; © Dave Stamboulis/Alamy; (cl) blickwinkel/Alamy; (cr) © Jeff Greenberg/Alamy; (bl) © David Burton/Alamy; (br) © Manor Photography/alamy; **12** Gandee Vasan/Stone/Getty Image; **12-13** ©Blomingimage/Corbis; **14** (t) Courtesy MacMillan; (b) Courtesy Kirchoff Wohlberg; **26** (bkgd) ©Tony Tayor/San Antonio Zoo; (inset) ©Don Despain/www.rekindlephotos.com/Alamy; **27** (tl) © Scott Doll/San Antonio Zoo; (cr) Gandee Vasan/Ston/Getty Images; (br) Photodisc/Getty Images; **28** (inset) © GK Hart/Vikki Hart/Riser/Getty Images; **28-29** (bkgd) San Antonio Zoo; **29**

(inset) ©Tim Graham/The Image Bank/Getty Images; **34** (t) Edgardo Contreras/Getty Images; (b) Patrick Molnar/Getty Images; **35** (tl) © Photodisc/SuperStock; (tr) Alaskastock; (cl) © Tom Stewart/Corbis; (cr) David Young-Wolff/ Photo Edit; (bl) © Ronnie Kaufman/Age Fotostock; (br) Masterfile (Royalty-Free Div.); **36** Yellow Dog Productions/Getty Images; **38-52** Courtesy George Ancona; **54** © Stockbyte/Alamy; (tl) Digital Vision/Alamy; **55** (tr)© Jack Hollingsworth/Photodisc/Getty Images; **56** (b) © Digital Vision/Alamy; **57** (t) ©Stockbyte/SuperStock ; **62** (t) ©Ryan McVay/Getty Images; (b) Digital Vision/Getty Images; **63** (tl) Photodisc/Getty Images; (tr) © Tomakazu Yamada/Getty Images; (cl) © Jose Luis Pelaez/Stone/Getty Images; (cr) © Anne Ackermann/Taxi/Getty Images; (bl) © Rachel Husband/Alamy; (br) © Tom Stock/Stone/Getty Images; **64** © blickwinkel/Alamy; **66** (t) Courtesy MacMillan; (b) Courtesy Kirchoff Wohlberg; **78-79** © Gary Crabbe/age fotostock; **79** (b) © Darrell Gulin/Stone/Getty Images; **80** (bl) © Amanda Hall/Getty Images; (br) Photodisc/Getty Images; **80-81** (bkgd) Corel Stock/Photo Library; **86** (t) FABIO COLOMBINI MEDEIROS/Animals Animals - Earth Scenes; (b) John B Free/npl/Minden Pictures; **87** (tl) © Stephanie Pilick/dpa/Corbis; (tr) Getty Images; (cl) © Bilderbuch/Design Pics/Corbis; (cr) Michael & Patricia Fogden/Minden Pictures; (bl) © Tony Arruza/Corbis; (br) © Buddy Mays/Corbis; **88** © Bartomeu Borrell/age fotostock; **90** (t) Courtesy Harper Collins; (b) Courtesy Harry Bliss; **102** Birgid Allig/Getty Images; **102-103** © Getty Images; **104** © Getty Images; **122** (t) Arthur Tilley/Getty Images; (b) Daniel Dempster Photography/Alamy; **123** (tl) Richard Hutchings/Photo Edit; (tr) Sean Justice/Getty Images; (cl) Juniors Bildarchiv/Alamy; (cr) imagebroker/Alamy; (bl) Bill Losh/Getty Images; (br) Michael Newman/Photo Edit; **124** © Paul Hardy/Corbis; **162** (t) © Joseph Sohm/Visions of America/Corbis; (b) Peter Oxford/Minden Picturers; **163** (tl) ZIGMUND LESZCZYNSKI/Animals Animals - Earth Scenes; (tr) © Francesc Muntada/Corbis; (cl) STEVE EARLEY/Animals Animals - Earth Scenes; (cr) © NOEL LAURA/Corbis SYGMA; (bl) Gerry Ellis/Minden Pictures; (br) MICHAEL